THE
ELEPHANTS
IN THE
ROOM

THE
ELEPHANTS
IN THE
ROOM

An Excavation

MARTIN ROWE

LANTERN BOOKS • NEW YORK
A Division of Booklight Inc.

2013
Lantern Books
128 Second Place
Brooklyn, NY 11231
www.lanternbooks.com

Library of Congress Cataloging-in-Publication Data

Rowe, Martin.
The elephants in the room : an excavation / Martin Rowe.
pages cm
ISBN 978-1-59056-387-8 (pbk. : alk. paper) —
ISBN 978-1-59056-388-5 (ebook)
1. Environmental protection—Kenya. 2. Wildlife conservation—
Kenya. 3. Human–animal relationships—Kenya. 4. Kenya—History.
5. Great Britain—Colonies—Africa, East—Administration.
6. Sheldrick, Daphne, 1934– 7. Maathai, Wangari. I. Title.
TD171.5.K4R69 2013
333.72096762—dc23
2013018977

Permissions

For Mia, who was there

Contents

Acknowledgments

I would like to acknowledge the life and work of Professor Wangari Maathai and Dame Daphne Sheldrick, honor their dedication to the welfare and protection of those whom the powerful have long exploited and humiliated, and express my gratitude for their commitment to the preservation of the wild on this planet. It has also been a blessing to get to know Muta Mathai (whom I must thank for translating some Kiswahili); Waweru Mathai; and Wanjira Mathai, her husband Lars, and daughters Ruth and Elsa.

I want to extend my appreciation to Sangamithra Iyer for a conversation that stimulated my thinking about this project; to Judy Stone for her invaluable advice and work on the manuscript; and to Namulandah Florence for her many insights into the Kenyan context of Professor Maathai's life and political and environmental activities.

None of what I've written here would have been possible without the support and companionship of Mia

MacDonald, who made me aware of the horrors that we inflict on nonhuman animals and brought to my attention Wangari Maathai and her work. In these, and countless other ways, she has immeasurably enriched my life and deepened my understanding of the many complexities of the world.

The Elephants in the Room is a contribution to Human–Animal Studies (HAS) in general and to Lantern's series of books in HAS in particular, entitled *{bio}graphies*. This series explores the relationships between human and non-human animals through scholarship in the humanities, social sciences, and natural sciences viewed through the lens of autobiography and memoir, to deepen and complicate our perspectives on the other beings with whom we share the planet.

Author's Note

Changing fashions in orthography and pronunciation over the past century have meant that some words in *The Elephants in the Room* are spelled differently in quotations than in the main text. The African micro-nationality whom Willard Price refers to as the Watussi are more commonly known these days as the Tutsi, which is how I've chosen to name them. I've opted to use the more common spelling of Kikuyu rather than Gikuyu to describe one of the peoples and languages of the Central Highlands of Kenya. The Masai people are often spelled using a double "a" (Maasai), which is how I've decided to write the word; however, I've used the more common spelling of Masai Mara to delineate the region of Kenya known for the splendor of its wildlife.

Dame Daphne Sheldrick's talk, given on May 8, 2012, at the American Museum of Natural History, including the slideshow, introductions, and the question-and-answer session, is available at the AMNH's YouTube site

<http://www.youtube.com/user/AMNHorg/vid-
eos>, then search for "Sheldrick" or <www.youtube.
com/watch?v=PqgPEMlycrI&feature=plcp>   (accessed
June 18, 2013). You can read about the death of Lawrence Anthony, "The Elephant Whisperer," at: <http://
delightmakers.com/news/wild-elephants-gather-inexpli-
cably-mourn-death-of-elephant-whisperer/>   (accessed
June 18, 2013).   —*M.R.*

Introduction

Toying Architecturally with the Bones

ON THE EVENING of May 3rd, 2012, my partner, Mia, and I took the elevator to the fourth floor of the American Museum of Natural History in New York City. We'd been invited to a soirée to celebrate the publication of *Love, Life, and Elephants*, a memoir by Dame Daphne Sheldrick, matriarch of the David Sheldrick Wildlife Trust, which looks after orphaned baby elephants and rhinoceroses at its compound at the edge of Nairobi National Park in Kenya. The Trust rehabilitates the elephants and rhinos over many years before it releases them into Tsavo National Park, also in Kenya.

The elevator doors opened and we turned right, into the Paul & Irma Milstein Hall of Advanced Mammals in the Lila Acheson Wallace Wing of Mammals and Their Extinct Relatives, where we were immediately confronted by the skeletons of three proboscideans—*mammut america-*

num, *gomphotherium*, and *mammuthus*. As you might imagine, to walk past these animals on the way to a fundraiser for preserving their distant elephantine descendants presented a certain cognitive dissonance. Nor were these the only bone-houses on display. We encountered, assembled in neatly arranged glass cases, the ancient precursors of camels, pigs, rhinos, tapirs, tigers, sloths, marmots, armadillos, deer, and horses. According to panels near the entryway, these creatures had vanished between 30,000 and 10,000 years ago, likely from two main causes, both of which tolled a familiar, depressing bell. These animals had either died at the spear points of our predecessors, who during the Paleolithic era had spread in sizeable numbers throughout the continents, or they'd been unable to adapt to the warmer weather that signaled the end of the Ice Age and had died out.

The living mammals among us were herded into a circular room that overlooked Central Park, in the turret named after the late socialite and philanthropist Brooke Astor, third wife of Vincent, one of whose extinct relatives had once been the richest man in America. John Jacob Astor (1763–1848) had made his fortune in real estate and through the trafficking of the fur of beavers, whose ancestors we'd also strolled past. Attendees at this social occasion feasted on members of the families *phasianidae* (chickens) and *penaeidae* (shrimp), spring rolls, and assorted nuts. The Trust's U.S. board members greeted us and the actress Kristin Davis told us of her connection to Daphne Sheldrick, and how inspired she'd been by her work.

The chair of the U.S. board invited the guest of honor—a stocky, white-haired woman in her late seventies—to the dais. In clipped, flatly enunciated tones, Dame Daphne (she'd been knighted in 2006) thanked us for coming, marveled at how long it had taken for her to write her book, and expressed her hope that we'd continue our support of the Trust. After some more grazing, the assembly then migrated to the museum's IMAX Theater, where Dame Daphne narrated a slideshow that illustrated her life in her native Kenya, and the many species of animals with which she'd been "privileged" to spend time over the decades. Following her address, Dame Daphne accepted questions, and then moved from the theater to a table, where a long line of people waited for her to sign their copies of *Love, Life, and Elephants* amid the totem poles, masks, basketry, and dioramas of the Indians of the Northwest Coast of the Pacific Ocean.

*   *   *

In the course of over twenty years as a publisher, book publicist, and a writer, I've been to several events like Dame Daphne's: the grand hall, the pitch/lecture, and then the ritual signing of the printed work. These occasions have a comforting trajectory as your relationship with the speaker becomes increasingly intimate: the figure standing at the distant podium; the hero sitting across a desk as she inscribes your copy; the writer whispering her words into your brain as you read. I thought such events had lost their ability to surprise me or challenge me to examine my various relationships with authors and the written word. But this evening caught me in a peculiar state of mind, one framed by loss and remembrance, with its own echoes of Africa and the call to protect the planet's resources.

Fourteen years previously, in the same theater, I'd attended a discussion between the American journalist Bill Moyers and a Kenyan woman as redoubtable and inimitable as Daphne Sheldrick: Professor Wangari Maathai. Founder of the Green Belt Movement (GBM), the organization that to date has planted over fifty million trees throughout Kenya, Prof (as many called her, with respect and affection) had been invited to the museum to close a series of conferences on religion and ecology developed at the Center for the Study of World Religions at Harvard University. I'd been to a couple of these meetings and had heard of Prof's work. So, I decided to go.

By the late 1990s, Prof was well known within international development circles as an environmentalist, a campaigner for political pluralism and human rights, and a champion of social justice. She'd begun GBM in 1977 as an outgrowth of the work that she'd undertaken earlier that decade with the National Council of Women of Kenya (NCWK) and the Environment Liaison Centre in Nairobi. Rural women had told her it was becoming more and more difficult to find wood for fuel and fencing, and harvest yields were down. They lamented that the rivers of Kenya's Central Highlands were becoming clogged with silt, shrinking, or drying up altogether.

Prof could see that these women were malnourished and not thriving, and it puzzled her. She'd been born and had spent much of her childhood in the region. Her community had had enough food to eat. Although a timber industry was in operation and acres burned for farming and ranching, forests still covered hillsides and water was plentiful. The solution for Prof was obvious: to plant more trees. The Green Belt Movement grew from Prof's personal response to deforestation into a program of the NCWK, and thence to a separate organization.

Within a few years of starting GBM, Prof realized that behind the problems of environmental degradation and the destructive agricultural practices of the rural poor—a symptom itself of deficient extension services to educate farmers about growing food, conserving topsoil, and protecting natural resources—lay a more profound, systemic failure. By the early 1980s, the great promise that awaited Kenya after it achieved independence from the British in December 1963 had been thwarted by corruption and a loss of civil liberties. Under the autocratic leadership of President Daniel arap Moi, whose regime was buttressed by the West amid the *realpolitik* of the Cold War (with Kenya seen as a bulwark against communism), the one-party political system had become increasingly oppressive and Kenya was stagnating. The aspirations and everyday lives of a disempowered populus were too often subject to the whims of a predatory and ruthless governing elite.

Prof began to develop consciousness-raising seminars she called Civic and Environmental Education (CEE), which for her formed the foundation of the tree-planting program. Trees became an entry point, as she would put it, to talk about larger issues of good governance and the commitment to protect public land, neither of which was being honored by politicians. Instead, Prof argued, they were dividing plots up among their friends, misusing or even stealing the resources they held in trust for the people, and inhibiting voices calling for the country to take a different direction. These elites retained their power by pitting against one other what Prof preferred to call "micro-nationalities" (rather than the pejorative word "tribes," which suggested a society with limited economic and cultural development).

The task for ordinary people, Prof argued in the CEE seminars, was to recognize what she called (employing an analogy that ordinary Kenyans would understand) "The Wrong Bus Syndrome." The people had been taken for a ride, ran the metaphor. They not only needed to recognize they were on the road to nowhere, but they had to summon the courage to ask the man who sat behind the wheel of state to account for the course he was charting and demand that he turn the bus around and head in the right direction. Even better, she said, the people should take over the bus and change the driver.

As a result of her efforts at "conscientization," to use the concept developed by the Brazilian educational theorist Paulo Freire, Prof and the Green Belt Movement became associated in Kenya and abroad with opposition to Moi's rule. Prof had been a figure of notoriety for some time in Kenya. She went through a very public divorce in the 1970s. She was also subject to a politically motivated ouster at the University of Nairobi in the early 1980s. In the course of her high-profile campaigns through the next two decades against one-party rule, arbitrary detention, and the illegal annexation or acquisition of public land by private persons or entities, Prof was arrested and jailed, verbally and physically assaulted, and publically humiliated and harassed by the ruling party and its cronies, who proclaimed her a rebellious and "un-African" woman who didn't know her place.

By the time I saw Prof at the museum, the situation in Kenya had become easier for her. The return of multipartism in the mid-1990s offered the hope that if the fractious opposition could unite (a task at which it had failed before and did not achieve for several more years), Moi's government was doomed. In 2002, the challengers finally came together for the parliamentary and presidential elections that took place that December. The Moi administration was defeated and Prof was voted in by an overwhelming majority as a Member of Parliament for the constituency of Tetu, which included her home village of Ihithe. She was also appointed an assistant minister for the environment in the new government, led by President Mwai Kibaki.

These events were, however, months in the future when, in 2001, Mia and I took a trip to Kenya with a human-development organization called World Neighbors. For a week, we visited the non-profit's projects in

Mwingi and Kitui districts, regions far removed from Mombasa's beaches or the comfortable lodges of the wildlife reserves. Negotiating rutted roads and dry riverbeds, trying to avoid potholes and trucks that barreled along the highways, our four-by-four pitched and rolled from dusty village to dusty village. There we heard from beekeeping collectives, inspected the wares of basket-weaving cooperatives, examined sand dams, toured under-furnished clinics, and sat in the empty classrooms of half-completed schools—trying to work out just what it was these earnest and unfailingly gracious men and women, who'd dressed in their best to present their report from this-or-that location or sub-location committee, expected us to do, beyond offering our unsolicited and perhaps unhelpful advice, buying their products, or funding a few solar panels to provide energy to a clinic or two.

One of our guides and translators, a tough-minded local woman named Christine Kilalo, ensured that our trip wasn't simply poverty tourism by giving us a crash course in the dilemmas of development that these communities faced: How would they establish satisfactory quality control for their goods and get them into the international marketplace? What should they prioritize in their budgets to distinguish between "wants" and "needs"? How should they apportion labor between the sexes, given what work was and wasn't considered socially acceptable for men and women to do? How would they maintain and buy spare parts for a complex piece of machinery they wanted, should the donor agency honor their request for it? And how would they manage the sometimes-fraught relationship between funder and beneficiary?

These questions lingered in our minds as, in the second week, we experienced the more conventional pleasures of a safari in the Masai Mara, where on the plains familiar to anyone who's seen a nature documentary on television we encountered vast herds of wildebeest and zebra, as well as lions, giraffes, elephants, water buffalo, cheetahs, and leopards. We also visited Nairobi National Park and the Sheldrick orphanage and watched the infant elephants and rhinoceroses as they were fed from huge baby bottles and kicked around a soccer ball to the delight of local schoolchildren and the other tourists with us. (The Trust opens its gates to the public between eleven o'clock and noon each morning.)

Before we traveled to Kenya, it had been suggested to me that I should contact the Green Belt Movement and ask if Wangari Maathai had a manuscript about her work or life that she wanted published. We arranged for a meeting with her in bustling, downtown Nairobi at the Stanley Hotel, named after the infamous explorer Henry Morton Stanley (1841–1904), and fabled watering hole for Ernest Hemingway, the future King Edward VIII of England, and other icons of a time when glamour and power in East Africa were concentrated in white hands loaded with liquor and/or ammunition. As we waited for Prof, a glance around the lobby at the large, red-faced men in suits shaking hands and sitting down to conduct business in various English accents suggested that not as much had changed as one might have imagined from the days when the only black people inside the Stanley were carrying a bag or tray for the *wazungu*—the somewhat contemptuous Kiswahili word for white people that can be literally translated as "lost souls."

A murmur and a craning of necks alerted us to the arrival of a middle-aged black woman of medium height, wearing a *kitenge* and striding purposefully through the doorway of the hotel. As she made her way toward us, Wangari Maathai unfurled the dazzling smile and effortless charisma that I'd seen in 1998 and was to experience on countless instances in the future. I noticed how warmly she greeted the porters, waiters, and support staff as well as the wannabe tycoons and politicos whom they were serving at the tables in the attached restaurant—and how the *wananchi* (Kiswahili for "ordinary folk") responded to her with awe and affection.

Prof welcomed us to Nairobi and introduced us to a man accompanying her—a compactly built, wary individual by the name of Dr. John Makanga, who disconcertingly remained silent for the duration of our meeting. We discovered later he was a pharmacist and one of the founders of the Mazingira Green Party in Kenya. On several occasions he'd protected Prof when her life had been threatened and had more than once been badly beaten up by state-sanctioned thugs.

It turned out that Prof did indeed have a manuscript—a "booklet," as she called it. I offered to make it available in the United States for her to sell when she came to America to fundraise. After mulling over the offer for several months, Prof agreed, and in 2003 my company, Lantern Books, published *The Green Belt Movement: Sharing the Approach and the Experience.*

During our meeting at the Stanley Hotel, Mia and I urged Prof to write her autobiography. People needed to hear her story, we told her. We knew she didn't have the time to sit down and write such a work, we continued, but we could record her thoughts and build up a manuscript that she could edit, an altogether easier task than composing from scratch. She thought this a practical solution, and so on the few occasions over the next three years that Prof came to the States and Mia went to Kenya on work for various human-development agencies, we'd tape her. In fact, on October 8, 2004, Mia was doing just that—sitting beside Prof with the recorder on as the car took them to a constituency meeting in Nyeri, Kenya, when Prof's cell phone rang and a Norwegian official informed her that she'd been awarded the Nobel Peace Prize. In January 2005, Mia recalled the experience for a magazine I co-founded, *Satya*:

> I turned to her and in typical semi-articulate American fashion said, "That is amazing. I'm so happy for you. Wow." I was dumbstruck. So was she, but just for a moment. She smiled broadly and then we hugged for what seemed like a long time. Her assistant, Alex, in the seat in front of us, had a broad smile on his face. As we moved apart, Maathai said, softly, "I didn't know anyone

was listening." There were tears in her eyes, the first I'd ever seen.

Prof could have asked the driver to turn the car around and head back to Nairobi, where the world's press was waiting, but characteristically she decided to postpone international fame for a few hours and keep her appointment with her constituents, for whom the Nobel meant nothing and who may have traveled a long way for the assembly. The car did, however, stop en route at the Outspan Hotel in Nyeri, where Mia took the opportunity to phone me in Brooklyn and wake me with the news.

Every publisher wishes for such a moment: that an author whose work and vision you believe in receives her or his due, and that their voice now has the opportunity to be heard by a much wider audience. Only five years after our founding, that moment had occurred for Lantern. As I absorbed what had happened, it was also clear to me that, although *The Green Belt Movement*'s sales would increase dramatically following this announcement (to Prof's and Lantern's obvious advantage), the autobiography could command an advance that Lantern didn't have the means to pay. Prof, in fact, shortly thereafter acquired the services of a publishing agent, and at that point could quite reasonably have dropped Mia and me from the project. After all, we had no contract, and the taping was still at an early stage. Prof had no real way of assessing our merits as writers or collaborators. Nevertheless, she let her agent know that since Mia and I had suggested the autobiography in the first place and had already gotten involved, we should be presented with the opportunity to put together a proposal. And so we did.

The agent accepted our proposal, which was bought by Knopf, and work began on what became *Unbowed: A Memoir.* There were the usual misunderstandings, false starts, and moments of doubt that cloud arrangements such as these. We were new at this, and so was she. Prof had hoped dearly to write the book entirely by herself, a task she knew in her heart was now impossible due to the even greater constraints on her time—such as parliamentary activity and the opportunities offered by the Nobel—than when we'd mentioned the autobiography in 2001. Invitations flooded in; tours beckoned. It was hard to find time to be with her; others pressed their favors and demands. The email inbox filled and then overflowed; there were speeches to make, ceremonial trees to plant, and donors, dignitaries, and celebrities to handle—all a function of the crazy world of instant and intense global renown. We tried not to take more of her day than was necessary, but we weren't too abashed to be the people for whom, on occasion, Prof would turn off her cell phone and hand to a staff member so we wouldn't be interrupted.

Like Dame Daphne, Prof held a signing, for *Unbowed* at the American Museum of Natural History, in 2006. Two further books followed: *The Challenge for Africa* (2008) and *Replenishing the Earth* (2010). Over the years, Mia helped Prof craft a number of op-eds and my company re-made and maintained the Green Belt Movement's website.

Other highlights were being present at the Nobel Prize festivities in Oslo, hosting members of Prof's family at our house, flying to Kenya (and other parts of the world) to work on the manuscripts with her, and the three of us talking at great length about a whole host of issues. Mia and I were among the friends in New York City who said goodbye to Prof in February 2011 as she traveled back to Kenya following medical treatment for the cancer that would take her life a few months later.

In September 2011, Mia, by then on the board of the Green Belt Movement–U.S., visited Kenya to attend the memorial ceremonies. Two months later, back in the country for a board meeting, Mia tried to take Prof's daughter, Wanjira, and granddaughter Ruth to the David Sheldrick Wildlife Trust to see the feeding of the baby elephants and rhinos. Unfortunately, the Nairobi traffic—despairingly called "The Jam" by city dwellers—made it impossible. "Time is running," Prof would say as she bustled out of a room to another engagement, for which she was invariably late. Somehow it seemed consonant with our experience of always playing catch-up in Prof's presence that the three generations of Kenyan women never made it to the orphanage while Prof was still alive.

*   *   *

In the eight months between Prof's death and Dame Daphne's lecture at the museum, I hadn't been able to gauge Prof's impact on my life or the nature of my grief at her passing. I'd been deeply involved in planning a memorial ceremony for her in New York City in November 2011, but I knew this commemoration wasn't an adequate laying to rest of my feelings or satisfactory frame for my thoughts about her. My immersion in Prof's life and work over ten years had been so concentrated, even passionate, that it seemed unimaginable that it should end, and so abruptly, within a year of her being diagnosed with cancer. The work was not yet done; something remained to be said beyond *thank you* and *farewell.*

In the days following Dame Daphne's book signing, I found myself thinking about my serendipitous connection with these two women and their books and the museum. Part of my search for the ties that bound them together was no doubt simply a reaction to the museum itself as a *memento mori*: a place that enshrined the passing of animate beings into history, the slow accretion of layers of time and soil over the wasted bodies of flora and fauna. Part of it was an attempt to combine in some fashion the work of these women whom I admired deeply, at a time when I was trying to weave together facets of my life as an environmentalist and animal advocate. Part of it was an effort to understand what place words themselves might have in setting a record straight, or making a case, or acting as their own memorials—even to the extent that every physical book (even one on recycled paper) was in essence the carcass of a tree, and that for the book to reach the widest audience it would need to be shipped around the world using the decomposed bodies of countless other flora and

fauna from the millennia before any of Paul and Irma Milstein's advanced mammals existed.

I asked myself what drew me to Prof and Dame
Daphne. Yes, their drive and passion, courage and conviction inspired me. But, accurately or not, I sensed that
behind their forthrightness and singularity lay a loneliness,
even a desperation, as they tried to resist the tide of glo-
balization, confront the short-termism and expediency of
public officials and those who elected them, and channel
more productively the economic hopes and desires of the
planet's more than seven billion people, whose ordinary,
even legitimate aspirations were decimating the natural
world these women loved so deeply and that provided
them with such solace. Would we ignore Prof's legacy and
continue to destroy the forests, thereby hastening another
climatic shift as devastating and destructive as the previous Ice Age? Were Dame Daphne's elephants and rhinos
doomed to end up like the other *mammalia* encased in
every corner of the museum—victims, as they had been
thousands of years earlier, of global warming and a growing,
rapacious human population, with its hunger for natural
resources, including members of the *phasianidae* (poultry),
suidae (pigs), and *bovidae* (cattle) families that were in turn,
according to the Food and Agriculture Organization of
the United Nations, contributing almost twenty percent
of greenhouse gases to the atmosphere?

Although I saw no clear method by which to knit their
stories together or answer these questions, that evening at
the museum had placed in proximity a number of issues

of great importance to me. I needed to sort out what I felt and feel out what I sorted. I imagined myself like an elephant coming across a pile of bones, slowly rolling my trunk over their smooth surfaces, attempting to both identify and remember the half-familiar ideas that had once been enfleshed. I knew I had not merely to examine these women's biographies but to do the same with my own privileged and particular history, as a privately educated Englishman with ties to Africa. I had to dig into the curious ways we in the West have viewed the forests and the natural world, and how we think of preserving living things and commemorating what has passed. There needed to be some kind of a reckoning, a settling of accounts, for what had been done in the name of Science and Progress and Civilization.

Above all, I would have to confront a number of elephants: from the actual creatures we continue to slaughter, the bones of whose ancestors were stitched together in the Hall of Extinct Mammals, to the metaphorical ones that are apparent now but were, despite their seeming unavoidability, once invisible . . . and even now are hard to meet head-on: the poisonous prejudices of racism, the troubling legacies of empire, and the noxious assumptions of patrimony and misogyny. I also needed to look at that other elephantine quality, memory, and more particularly of the evasions and occlusions that occur when any of us try to tell our stories or those of others, and the fantasies we project onto the "other."

The Elephants in the Room is the result of that investigation. Like all excavations, this one began partly on a hunch that something interesting lurked beneath the placid surface of the everyday. Like all excavations, *Elephants* tries to piece together the uncovered fragments to match a set of pre-existing beliefs and stories that could be wrong, misidentified, and misleading. Yet it's my belief that these shards are worth dusting down, if only to encourage further analysis and invite different arrangements that may offer more convincing narratives of how we came to be where we are. Like an elephant, the book itself will range far—into the forests, upriver, and across the continents—a beast of burden, hauling its metaphors like logs, carrying within its body memories of warfare and kindness, promises broken and fulfilled, and dreams of a future shadowed by the mistakes and illusions of the immediate and distant past.

And it is with the immediate and distant pasts of Daphne Sheldrick and Wangari Maathai that we begin.

1

The Noble Cause

IN 1887, A commercial association—the Imperial British East Africa Company—leased a strip of coastal land from the Sultan of Zanzibar, in one of the first proprietary acts of the European colonization of a region that ultimately became Kenya, Tanzania, and Uganda. A decade later, after the failure of the company had required the transfer of its responsibilities to the imperial government, the British decided to open up the interior to possible trade from the coast to the inland lake that the British explorer John Hanning Speke (1827–1864) named after Victoria, Queen of the United Kingdom and Ireland and Empress of India. The local colonial administration commissioned the building of a railway from Mombasa, on the Indian Ocean, to Kisumu five hundred miles inland, and shipped in indentured labor from the Indian subcontinent to perform the task. The construction lasted five years, cost hundreds of millions of dollars, and took almost 2,500 lives.

It's at this time and within a *topos* familiar to all empires—a grandiose project, magnificent in its madness and appalling in the costs it exacts, conceived of by one people and built by others whom it's effectively enslaved—that *Love, Life, and Elephants* begins. We start with Dame Daphne's Great-Uncle Will, whose ancestors departed Scotland for Africa in the mid-1820s. He was, writes the author, an enthusiastic big game hunter—so much so, that he would regularly board a steamship for Kenya from the Eastern Cape of South Africa, where he and his family lived, for just such purposes.

On one expedition early in the twentieth century, Will befriended Sir Charles Eliot (1862–1931), then governor of the British colony. Eliot had been ordered to expand the branch lines of the train route. During a hunt, writes Dame Daphne, Eliot made Will an offer: if he brought twenty families to settle in Kenya, the government would give them free farmland so they could foster trade and provide resources for the burgeoning railroad. Will thought this a splendid idea and easily made up the quota by persuading members of his own large and extended clan to join him. They set off, Dame Daphne writes, with "a nucleus of [farm animal] breeding stock, as well as farm implements, seeds, tools, furniture and most importantly, guns and ammunition to protect themselves and their property" (3). Once they reached Mombasa, they boarded the train to Nairobi, on a journey that took longer than strictly necessary. At regular intervals, Will felt the urge to stop the train to bag trophies—something that apparently didn't annoy the other passengers, who were content to "take part in the fun as spectators" (7).

At this early point in her narrative, Dame Daphne feels the need to draw attention to the obvious:

> How lightly my ancestors shot at animals. For us, now living in a different era, conscious of the decimation of wildlife and privileged even to glimpse such creatures in a wild situation, the actions of my forefathers appear shocking and difficult to understand. But at that time the maps of Kenya showed little on their empty faces, and beyond each horizon stretched another and another of endless untouched acres, sunlit plains of corn-gold grass, wooded luggas, lush valleys, crystal-clear waters. And everywhere there was wildlife in such spellbinding profusion that it is difficult for those who were never witness to this to even begin to visualize such numbers. At the time no one ever imagined that any amount of shooting could devastate the stocks of wild game, let alone all but eliminate it (6–7).

What Dame Daphne doesn't draw attention to is that the land that Charles Eliot promised the settlers was free only if you discounted the human and nonhuman animals who traversed it or made it their home, even if they were unable to draw up a written deed to the property. The maps of Kenya may have had "empty faces," but the lands they delineated were not void: they contained animals and people. Certainly, when the railroad was being built, the inhabitants of the area—from the Maasai and Nandi micro-nationalities to the man-eating lions who attacked and killed many laborers—expressed in their particular fashion a belief that this was their territory. Dame Daphne herself observes that Will and his kinfolk passed through locations that were clearly inhabited by human beings. They knew this because the tribeswomen would ululate and the men would sometimes launch spears at the wagons, "before Great-Uncle Will bravely stepped forward to appease the local people with calming gestures" (8).

Once the immigrants arrived at the places the British government had allotted to them, they spent months clearing the bush and setting up homesteads. Farming was a hard life to begin with, and the families discovered that the new surroundings didn't make it easier. Dame Daphne's great-grandparents, the Aggetts, found their property and its accompanying weather patterns and diseases unfavorable to growing crops and raising cattle. They decided to move. Other reasons, apart from access to more game, precipitated their departure:

[I]t had already dawned on the authorities that the isolated and vulnerable white settlers of Masailand would have to be moved elsewhere, and negotiations with the relevant elders and chiefs were already under way to bring the Masai people from around Kenya to the area around Narok so that they were settled in one place, away from their enemies, the Kikuyu. By the time Great-Grandpa arrived in Nairobi, the decision had already been taken to move him and his family out of Masailand, and offer them alternative holdings on the Laikipia Plateau. This was prize ranching country, where wildlife also abounded in numbers that matched the endless herds of the Athi plains and the Masai lands of Narok (13).

Wangari Maathai was a Kikuyu who was born in 1940, and she records this period at the turn of the twentieth century differently. Prof didn't know her great-grandparents, but she writes in *Unbowed* that they would have inhabited a world virtually untouched by Europeans. They would also have lived isolated from other ethnic communities, except for the Maasai, who'd raid Kikuyu villages for cattle and occasionally kill young men, as Kikuyus would the Maasai. Prof takes pains to mention that the skirmishes weren't constant: "There were also times of truce, trade in the form of exchange of food, livestock, and land, and even intermarriage." Where she was born, near Nyeri in the Central Highlands,

mixed Maasai and Kikuyu blood was common and never viewed as a stigma. My mother had Maasai blood in her. . . . We were told that my great-great-grandmother on my father's side was a Maasai who was abducted during a raid. When she came to the highlands, she adopted

Kikuyu customs and named her second son Muta, after her father. That name was eventually handed down to my father and, later, to my second son (7–8).

Prof also recalls the types of "negotiations" that Dame Daphne discusses, suggesting that the relocation of Kenya's micro-nationalities may have had less altruistic purposes than reducing conflict between ethnic groups:

> The settlers received title deeds to most of the land in areas where they preferred to settle, near emerging city centers or regions that seemed promising for successful wheat, maize, coffee, and tea farming, and for grazing livestock. To make way for them, many people were displaced, including a large number who were forcibly relocated to the Rift Valley. Those who refused to vacate their land were transported by the British elsewhere (9).

By the time Prof's father, Muta, and mother, Wanjiru, were born (in 1903 and 1906 respectively), Christianity and the colonial administration were embedded in the Central Highlands. Prof's parents were baptized as adults, and when he came of age, Muta joined some 150,000 other Kikuyu men in migrating from the native reserves—those parts of the country set aside for them by the British—to white-owned farms, where they effectively became squatters. The move was an economic necessity for men such as Muta, since the British were determined to pay for local development by raising revenue within the country and had decided against using the existing currency, which was an exchange of goats. Prof continues:

> They also wanted to create a labor force, but they did not want to force people to work. So they introduced an income tax for men in most parts of the country that could be paid only in the form of money. . . . Of course, the colonial government and the British settlers were the only ones with money in their hands. So the local people, especially men, were indirectly forced to work on settlers' farms or in offices so they could earn money to pay taxes. By the 1940s, settlers' farms constituted a major source of employment (13–14).

Muta went off in search of work, and in 1943, Prof and her mother joined him in Nakuru in the Rift Valley on the farm of a white settler, D. N. Neylan. Muta owned no land of his own, but was apportioned part of the property where he could grow crops.

*   *   *

In 1934, the year of Dame Daphne's birth, His Majesty's East African Trade and Information Office published *Kenya: Britain's Most Attractive Colony*, a work I stumbled across as I was sorting out my late aunt's house and property a few months into writing this book—another happy accident in a host of strange coincidences in 2012 that insisted I make connections among them. The purpose of the brochure, runs the foreword, was "to convey to those who know little of Kenya an informative picture of a country which is progressive and progressing, but which, in its emergence from obscurity, has retained its own peculiar charm."

One might question just how obscure the land known as Kenya was to the peoples who lived in it, let alone the Arabs who sailed along its coasts and had raided the interior for hundreds of years. The editors of *Kenya* are unconcerned with such niceties. They outline how Great Britain first cast its benign gaze upon the region, when, "at the request of the reigning chief," a protectorate was established over Mombasa, which by the final quarter of the nineteenth century was the center of the slave trade run by the notorious Hamad bin Muhammad bin Jumah bin Rajab bin Muhammad bin Saʻīd al-Murghabī, more pithily known in the West as Tippu Tip (1837–1905).

Kenya: Britain's Most Attractive Colony claims that it took over eighty years of British effort to suppress the slave trade along the coast of the Indian Ocean, "which she did unaided by any other Western power. As a result of circumstances arising from this beneficent work, our nation, which had previously refused to assume protection, was forced to undertake the control of the country in 1895. East Africa became British East Africa." The pamphlet goes on to describe the colonization of the land throughout the next two decades, including in 1904 "a large party of settlers from South Africa," and the "soldier settlement scheme" of a decade and a half later, through which "many new settlers of the right type arrived in the Colony."

Not surprisingly, given its purpose, *Kenya* presents a very rosy picture of the country—one whose resources were not so much wrested from the original inhabitants but given up without a fight by Nature herself to those intelligent enough to grasp her superfluity: "[Vasco da Gama] would be still more amazed by the wealth which prodigal Nature has yielded to white settler and tutored African in the hinterland." It's a land free of malaria, where just about all settlers (including the women) are "virile," tuberculosis rates are low, and even new arrivals over the age of sixty "have shown a remarkable rejuvenation of ability and capabilities." The booklet offers glowing reports on the province's transportation, mining, agriculture, and other industries, and in a section entitled "Women's Work" issues encouraging words on social life and the forming of charitable associations and guilds to help recent immigrants. Advertisements detail bustling commerce and trade in coffee, sisal, wheat, maize, coconuts, sheep, and a host of other products and services. We're advised in the "Social Life" chapter that "the people of Kenya treasure their reputation for hospitality.... They welcome the stranger with all the traditional kindness and good nature characteristic of so many English, Scottish, Irish, Welsh and Dominion homes."

Little in evidence throughout a volume extolling the attractions of the colony is any in-depth information about the original "people of Kenya." We're told that Africans, by which is meant *black* Africans, are especially enthusiastic shoppers, drinkers, and smokers of cigarettes and that both African men and woman "are glad to supplement the returns from their own produce by wages earned in the [white] 'settled areas.'" Every now and again a photograph will display groups of African micro-nationalities. Nonetheless, the document is clearly touting an Africa where the natives are decorative consumers or eager laborers for a productive and committed white community freed of the burdens of lassitude and self-doubt.

By the second and third decades of the twentieth century, Dame Daphne's ancestors (who appear from *Love, Life, and Elephants* to be exactly what *Kenya: Britain's Most Attractive Colony* had in mind as "settlers of the right type") were flourishing. Her uncles and aunts were "setting up professional hunting parties, cattle-ranching establishments, farms, hotels, transport and trading companies" (14). Dame Daphne's parents possessed a typical colonial home with "large symmetrical bay windows" that opened to a "gorgeous garden and spectacular views and [were] joined by a spacious verandah." In addition,

[a] small high opened window overlooked the woodpile outside, where, once a week, the African wives of workers on the farm brought a load of wood on their backs in exchange for a weekly portion of maize-meal and the two-acre plot on the farm for each family of workers, which they could cultivate and where they could graze a maximum of thirty goats and sheep (21).

Prof's home on Mr. Neylan's farm was also typical: in this case, a Kikuyu homestead known as a *thingira*. Her father had his own hut, constructed of mud and wood with a roof of grass thatch, while each of his four wives had a residence, or *nyũmba*, which was between "twenty and thirty feet across and divided into several separate areas by walls or sticks." Prof writes:

> My mother had her own place to sleep, while my sisters and I slept together in our own compartment, as my brothers did in theirs. Our beds were wood planks topped by mattress covers that we stuffed with leaves, ferns, and grass.
>
> The houses had no electricity or running water and were dark inside. There were small windows, but with no glass in them (17).

On Mr. Neylan's farm, Prof writes, the various ethnicities worked on separate tasks: the Kikuyus in the field, the Luos around the homestead, and the Kipsigis with the livestock. They lived separately and rarely spoke each others' languages. Indeed, "except for the skin color we shared we were as 'foreign' to one another as the British settlers were to us. I grew up knowing that I was a Kikuyu and that the other communities were different from us." There were the inevitable ethnic biases, which, she observes, were "planted early in one's childhood, [and] became amplified and were embraced by national political rhetoric. They are still used today to divide Kenyans from one another" (22–23). Prof never talked to Mr. Neylan, his wife, or his daughter, although she says that over the years her father and Mr. Neylan grew to be friends, or "as good friends as a master and his employee can be." When Kenya achieved independence, Mr. Neylan gave Muta twenty-five acres of the farm. Muta then joined a cooperative with other workers and bought Mr. Neylan out.

*   *   *

Beyond its florid description of Vasco da Gama's coastal explorations and Britain's heroic ending of the Arab slave trade, *Kenya: Britain's Most Attractive Colony* doesn't dwell on what it admits is the Kenya colony's "colourful" history, before Britannia arrived to settle everything and everyone down with its own particular version of Great-Uncle Will's calming gestures. "The past has not been forgotten," the handbook assures its readers, "if only because the present has sprung out of it, but the main endeavour has been to outline Kenya as it is to-day, the product of just over thirty years of effective British influence." It was in such a world, where the colonial administration had determined that the *significant* past was merely a few decades old, that Wangari Maathai grew up. It was only through conversing with her elders and in her own independent study later on that she became aware not merely of her land's "colourful" history, but of a pre-Christian and pre-colonial Kikuyu polity that possessed its own systems of governance and rituals, which sustained the community's self-identity and culture and gave people's lives shape and texture. It's not too much to say that her recovery of this legacy animated a substantial portion of her life's work.

Prof was always scrupulous in how she examined the different legacies of colonialism as they affected her country, the peoples who lived within its borders, her family, and her own life. For instance, in her writing and in many speeches she expressed her gratitude to the Irish and Italian nuns who educated her at the Catholic boarding schools she went to after four years at the local primary school. She was in awe at their dedication to teaching girls and young women in a land so far from their own, and she honored their commitment to a mission greater than any desire they may have had for a family, fame, or simply to live nearer home.

Yet Prof was also deeply conscious of how the Christian missionaries who arrived in Kenya in the mid- to late nineteenth century had demonized the rituals and religious practices of the peoples of the Central Highlands. The oral culture of Kikuyus, she wrote, proved no match for the written word of the Bible, especially as it was accompanied by modern medicine and weaponry. Within a few decades, virtually everyone in that region had embraced "modernity," which meant learning to read the Bible (which was the first book translated into Kikuyu), adopting Western dress, and embracing Christianity.

For Prof, the colonial forces' attempt to demolish an existing cultural identity was a deliberate ploy to end resistance and instill passivity. If you had something to believe in, you fought; if you had nothing worth protecting, you gave in; if you believed that what replaced your culture was superior or offered you a personal advantage, you not only acquiesced in its destruction but you hastened its demise and enforced that process by attacking those among you who resisted. Prof spoke to Mia and me eloquently and with a focused anger about those she called "collaborators": local people who, by taking up positions in the regional government during the colonial period, had joined forces with the British to undermine the independence of the various micro-nationalities.

The African peoples' inability to chart their own destinies and failure to maintain the values that sustained their cultures were, for Prof, *the* fundamental reasons why so many communities in the continent south of the Sahara hadn't thrived. That loss was linked very closely in Prof's mind with environmental destruction. Kikuyus, she wrote, like other peoples who lived in the Central Highlands, oriented their lives toward Mount Kenya (known, before it was "discovered" by two German explorers, as Kirinyaga, or "Place of Brightness"). They buried their dead with their heads pointing toward the mountain; their doors faced it; religious ceremonies took place upon its slopes; and God was thought to live upon it. Because the mountain was sacred, its ecological functions remained intact. When the missionaries arrived, they told the peoples of the Central Highlands that God didn't live on the mountain but should only be worshipped in church. Prof commented mordantly that every Sunday the descendants of those first Christians filed into those same churches, built with trees cut from the hillsides, to pray for rain, which was less likely to occur because of the deforestation.

The establishment of a cash economy under the British depended on the extraction of natural resources, such as timber, and the growing of commodity crops, such as tea and coffee, which the British encouraged. (*Kenya: Britain's Most Attractive Colony* contains a photograph called "Kenya Forest" in which hundreds of logs are depicted prone before a shrinking woodland in the background.) Over the decades, settlers and local people degraded the environment of Mount Kenya and other mountain ranges by cutting down the trees that held dirt in place, stored moisture in their root system, and encouraged clouds to form through evapotranspiration. Topsoil reddened the crystal-clear rivers that both Prof and Dame Daphne describe in their books. The clouds dispensed less rainwater and fewer trees conserved it, which meant that the land dried out and the streams shrank.

This desiccation, for Prof, was the inevitable consequence of a mindset that desacralized the natural world in favor of a transcendent, heavenly life that would welcome the true believer after he or she had passed through this vale of tears, and/or placed immediate economic and material welfare over long-term sustainability, or indeed survival. As she wrote in *Replenishing the Earth* (93–97), colonial forces often destroyed groves sacred to native peoples both to demoralize the local peoples and to access the riches therein. Although Prof understood the impulses that made *wananchi* hope for a better life beyond the difficult one immediately before them, she couldn't understand why they didn't see that their practices were making their life on Earth so much harder and more painful.

This combination of social, moral, and ecosystemic consciousness was the driving force behind Prof's activism. She aspired to create an intimate and self-sustaining virtuous cycle between a people and their immediate environment. The consequence of the destruction of the culture was that a micro-nation (indeed, *any* micro-nation) that had been self-confident and independent, and although poor not impoverished (a crucial distinction), became alienated from its own livelihood, bioregion, and identity. It became weak and dependent: easy prey to the blandishments and empty promises of politicians; occasionally surly and ungrateful recipients of foreign aid; active destroyers of their own resource base; and passively reliant for their future on an unstable, commodified economy run by a powerful and distant elite.

*   *   *

Following the end of World War II, during which Dame Daphne's father had been ordered to arrange the killing of thousands of zebras and wildebeest to feed British and Kenyan troops and Italian prisoners of war in Abyssinia (now Ethiopia), independence movements sprang up or gained strength in colonial regimes around the world as the retreat from empire began. From 1952 to 1960, the

Kikuyus, Embus, and Merus rebelled in an insurgency that became known as the Mau Mau uprising.

Mau Mau—a phrase of uncertain origin, but believed by some to be taken from the sound of the secret vows that bonded the warriors together—entailed, according to Dame Daphne, "[o]athing ceremonies involving obscene rituals . . . often imposed under duress, some said to be so barbaric that the details were spoken of only in hushed whispers. The increased attacks on the livestock and property of the white farmers, plus an escalation in lawlessness, were all symptoms" of a change in the country. For some among Dame Daphne's family and friends—"or any of us white Kenyans for that matter"—the idea, propounded by the Mau Mau rebels, that the settlers were illegal intruders was wrong. "Rather than brutal foreign colonizers," she writes with the vigor of H. M. East African Trade and Information Office, "we and our ancestors were humane and totally honourable pioneers who had braved the unknown and, with blood, sweat and toil, brought progress to darkest Africa, promising law and order and good governance under benign British rule" (50–51).

Dame Daphne notes that the warnings made "by those in the know" to quash the rebellion before it grew too large went unheeded by the British government. As a result,

the intimidation meted out by the activists against those who gave witness against the [Mau Mau] organization, or who refused to take the secret oath of allegiance,

became more brutal, barbaric and savage, with murder
and mutilation turning into almost daily events.

At first, everyday life was not radically affected, but
then as the evidence of carnage shifted—from strangled
cats and headless dogs hung from trees, to white farmers
brutally murdered—we had to restrict our movements.
No longer could we stay out in the forest, and doors
had to be locked by nightfall. My father moved his ped-
igree stock nearer the house and employed tribesmen
not aligned to the Kikuyu, Embu and Meru to guard
them at night (51).

In spite of these and other precautions, the extended
family did not go unharmed. Dame Daphne's grandparents, the Webbs, were robbed and beaten to unconscious-
ness by rebels and counted themselves lucky to escape with
their lives. They removed for their safety to their seaside
cottage in Malindi. Great-Aunt Ethel's farm was torched
and the black foreman, his wife, and their three children
were burned alive (58). A Mkamba worker for the family,
whom Dame Daphne's family nicknamed Kinanda ("the
gramophone") because he was always singing, expired
from heart-sickness. On his deathbed, writes the author,
he revealed that "[i]n an enforced Mau Mau oathing ceremony he had been ordered to murder us all, and because
he refused to do this, loving the family too much to kill us
in cold blood, a death curse was cast on him" (52). He had
turned it into a self-fulfilling prophecy.

The terror, notes Dame Daphne, affected many communities, not least Kikuyus loyal to the Crown, "of whom there were many" (56). The British troops sent to quell the rebellion proved no match for the Mau Mau insurgents, who were well acquainted with the forested terrain of the Central Highlands. Dame Daphne's then husband, Bill Woodley, also knew the land intimately, and he and her brother Peter went out on special operations to hunt down the rebels on behalf of the government. As it turned out, the skills that Bill honed chasing down the Mau Mau rebels in the forests stood him in good stead as he attempted to stop the poachers who were flooding the newly created Tsavo National Park (68).

At this point in *Love, Life, and Elephants*, the author switches from general observations about her community to more direct, personal declarations. Among the settler community, Dame Daphne writes,

[T]here was resentment at the overtly sympathetic views of many of the British servicemen towards the Mau Mau cause and their condemnation of us settlers as a privileged elite who had no real right to be in Kenya in the first place. I was deeply affected by this. I knew that I was British through and through and loyal to the Crown, yet here I was being stigmatized by my so-called countrymen. . . . Labelled the White Tribe of Africa, we were rapidly losing our stake in the country we viewed as home and could never be truly British again, due to long isolation in Africa. Nor could we be truly African either, because of colour and culture (56–57).

Through the 1950s, the British ratcheted up their efforts to defeat the Mau Mau. Bombers dropped their loads on suspected Mau Mau hideouts in the range of mountains known as the Aberdares—driving, according to Dame Daphne, the animals insane with anxiety at assaults that must have been baffling and terrifying to them. She is appalled at how the Mau Mau warriors destroyed populations of tree hyraxes, suni antelopes, and squirrels by wearing their skins and fur. The British authorities arrested Jomo Kenyatta (1893–1978), leader of the independence movement and later the first president of liberated Kenya, whom they considered the mastermind behind the rebellion. They sent Kenyatta into internal exile, and set up a series of encampments, surrounded by barbed wire and guard posts, in which entire communities were corralled. The British counter-offensive proved effective, and by the late 1950s, Dame Daphne writes, the "emergency" (as the British tersely called it) was winding down. Dedan Kimathi, the charismatic guerrilla leader, was caught and hanged in 1957, and only about 1,500 Mau Mau activists remained at large (68).

Wangari Maathai also lived through the Mau Mau rebellion, and her recollections of the period diverge in major ways from Dame Daphne's. As far as Prof was concerned, the rebellion's immediate cause lay not in strange cultic behavior but in the conscientization of African men who'd fought for the British in World War II. Much as African-Americans were awakened to the injustices that awaited them in the U.S. and began to agitate for their civil rights, East African men returned home to find the freedom they'd fought to protect for their colonial masters still beyond their own reach. "Not only did they not receive any recognition or compensation for their service," Prof writes, "but, to add insult to injury, their British colleagues were being showered with honors and even allocated land, some of it taken from the Kenyan war veterans, who were forcibly displaced" (61). These men were frustrated and they knew how to fight: the British had trained them well.

For Prof, however, the real source of the rebellion was a betrayal older than the allotment of land following either the first or second world war. The cause was an act of perfidy based on a very different reading of the history of her country than that found in *Kenya: Britain's Most Attractive Colony*. In 1890, at the very outset of British commercial interest in the region, Captain (later Lord) Frederick Lugard (1858–1945) had met a Kikuyu leader called Waiyaki wa Hinga (d. 1892). The aim of the parlay, Prof writes, was "to establish station posts for the Imperial British East Africa Company on Kikuyu land and enable goods to be brought to and from Uganda." The encounter, Prof continues, was momentous:

Lugard and Waiyaki swore an oath to allow the station posts on the condition that the British would not take Kikuyu land or other property. The agreement, however, did not last long, because Lugard's [non-Kikuyu] porters started looting the nearby settlements and raping women. The Kikuyus fought back in a series of battles that culminated in a standoff in 1892, when Waiyaki was captured, taken away, and eventually buried alive by the colonial administration (62).[1]

The Kikuyus were stunned by the treachery and shocked at how lightly the British had considered an oath that the Kikuyus took very seriously. "But as the Kikuyus would learn," Prof states, "the newcomers had no time for verbal promises between themselves and the native population. Eventually the strangers simply acquired and distributed land to themselves and others, who began arriving in Kenya in numbers" (62).

In *Unbowed*, Prof argues that the notion that Africans passively accepted colonialism is incorrect: everyone put up a fight at first (see also *Challenge* 36–37), but if they weren't appeased by the calming gestures of white men like Dame Daphne's Great-Uncle Will, they certainly were by the colonists' weaponry. The British administration, as we've seen, introduced taxes and the indirect forced labor necessary to pay for them, and accompanied it with a *kipande*, an identification system that required every black male in Kenya to carry a pass—a method, as under apartheid in South Africa, to monitor and control a population that might otherwise

---

1 A concise version of Waiyaki wa Hinga's life and death by Hannington Ochwada can be found in *Holy People of the World: A Cross-Cultural Encyclopedia*, edited by Phyllis G. Jestice (Santa Barbara, Calif.: ABC-CLIO, 2004), pp. 905–6.

rebel. When local men started to organize and campaign for better conditions, the British violently broke up a peaceful protest in 1922, and banned or curtailed African associations or periodicals (63).

As a dutiful child of Empire and the Church, Prof, then in Catholic boarding school, prayed to God every night to protect her and her fellow students from the Mau Mau. "The British propaganda kept us naïve about the political and economic roots of the conflict," she writes, "and was designed to make us believe that the Mau Maus wanted to return us to a primitive, backward, and even satanic past" (64).

Wanjiru, Prof's mother, was forced to live in an "emergency village," a kind of stockaded enclosure, where she stayed for nearly seven years. Even though she was carrying a pass, Prof herself was arrested by the British in Nakuru when she was about sixteen years old and thrown into a detention camp, mainly because, she writes, she was a Kikuyu in the wrong place at the wrong time: "The conditions were horrible—designed to break people's spirits and self-confidence and instill sufficient fear that they would abandon their struggle. Sanitation was poor, food was minimal, and the camp was very crowded" (67–68). Because she was dressed in her school uniform and, she suspects, through the offices of her father and Mr. Neylan, she was released after two days as no threat to anyone.

As was the case with Dame Daphne's relatives, the Mau Mau rebellion caused a great deal of discussion and sometimes schisms within Prof's family. Prof observes that her father had a high regard for Mr. Neylan, which made him suspect in the eyes of other family members (66). At one point in the conflict, Prof's father was sheltered from Mau Mau retribution by Mr. Neylan, and both of her older brothers were compelled by the British to join the Home Guards, a force made up of black Kenyans who operated as proxies for the British military. In effect, her brothers served alongside other Kikuyus who were, to use Prof's word, "collaborators."

As it did with Dame Daphne's family, violence hit close to Prof's home: the Mau Mau insurgents burned down a Home Guards' depot across the ridge from her village, killing more than twenty: "It was one of the worst local massacres by the Mau Mau and left many widows in the community. Such traumas have never been addressed. Indeed, there has almost been a desire to deny these atrocities took place. There is still need for healing, reconciliation, and forgiveness" (65). In her memoir, Prof insists that the initial Mau Mau rebellion had decent motives, which didn't involve the violation of women or extreme cruelty. However, as the war "deteriorated into internal strife between the Home Guards and Mau Maus, the barriers became blurred, [and] the Mau Maus started using tactics that could punish even the innocent" (65).

Prof takes issue with the idea that the white settlers were disproportionately affected by the violence. Referencing Caroline Elkins's *Imperial Reckoning* and David Anderson's *Histories of the Hanged*, she notes that only thirty-two white settlers were killed because of Mau Mau activities, as opposed to more than 100,000 Africans, mostly Kikuyus, who died in concentration camps and emergency villages, or who lost property and suffered trauma. Prof is laconic about the apportionment of blame for the atrocities: "It is clear that terrorism was not confined to one side" (68).

                •   •   •

In spite of these very dissimilar narratives of the same event, Daphne Sheldrick and Wangari Maathai shared a degree of alienation from the country that was to become the Republic of Kenya in December 1963. For Dame Daphne's older relatives, the British government's determination to grant Kenya independence and the decision that the form of the democracy would be "one man, one vote" were further blows to the pioneers. After all, half a century earlier the administration had invited those who lived under the Crown to come to this land and to forge a new way of life. They had built up the colony, so the settlers' reasoning went, and now they would either be forced out or would have no sway in determining the country's future, given that they were greatly outnumbered by the black Kenyans (119–120).

Prof also felt that Kenya as a nation was an unsatisfactory entity. She thought that the constitution that was imposed on the new state was a holdover from colonial times and didn't reflect the needs of the Kenyan people. In fact, for the remainder of her life, Prof campaigned for a constitution that more adequately responded to the diversity of Kenyan society and protected the natural resources of the country. Prof ultimately succeeded in having key provisions regarding these inserted into the new constitution, which, to her all-too-fleeting satisfaction, was ratified only a few weeks before she died.

In 1964 and beyond, however, as Prof writes in *Unbowed* and *The Challenge for Africa*, not only were Kenya's different micro-nationalities lumped together with other ethnic groups they may have had no connection with, but the country—like many newly independent states—made little attempt to address the wrongs of the past or to reorganize the power structure more equitably. The Mau Mau rebels were neither honored nor even properly remembered by the state. Indeed, Prof observes in *Unbowed* that "it is only very recently that the law in Kenya has been changed so that the Mau Maus are no longer described as *imaramuri* ('terrorists') but as freedom fighters" (68).

For Prof, this was yet another sign of how vital memory and sufficient recollection of one's history were to cultural survival. When she planted the first seven trees that began the Green Belt Movement, she did so in honor of important local men and women throughout Kenya's history who'd stood up for the interests of their peoples against the colonial forces.

Prof also found Kenya's post-independence politics not up to the task of bringing the country together and establishing a sound footing for long-term development. Jomo Kenyatta was far from the radical that the British portrayed him as. He sought to reassure the international community that he wouldn't seek redress for the British presence in Kenya. More seriously, successive governments made little attempt to revisit and resolve the loss of property and the contested apportionment of land that had occurred over the previous several decades because of the forced relocation of many Kenyans. This issue remained a lesion that would, over the next forty years, lead to violence among communities, particularly in and around the Rift Valley.

Prof argued that the failure to acknowledge the traumas of the past and the ad-hoc origination of many nation states in Africa—imperial powers drawing arbitrary lines on a map, throwing different ethnicities together, leaving countries at independence with limited or no capacity for self-governance—ultimately led to greater instability. In her view, the African state, far from providing a national identity that brought different communities together, was too often in effect a large cash register that different groups periodically fought over for a chance to raid.

As Mia and I worked with Prof on her books, we ourselves could see how the wounds of those times continued to fester. In 2008, a criminal gang called the Mungiki, dominated by Kikuyus and reputedly drawing upon Mau Mau oathing ceremonies to enforce internal and external terror in the informal settlements bordering downtown Nairobi, came to public attention when it was reported that they'd sent death threats to Prof because of her perceived opposition to the government, the head of which was a Kikuyu. Prof, who'd been urging the government to investigate not only the causes of Mungiki's violence but whether police death squads were systematically murdering suspected Mungiki members, suggested that the threats were in fact coming from government forces disguised as Mungiki.

When we asked her about this tangle of accusation and counter-accusation, Prof told us that the Mungiki outrages were the end consequence of decades of silence and dislocation for families following the Mau Mau rebellion, themselves a result of the century-long destruction by outside forces of local governance, male rites of passage, and micro-national cultural identity. Men and women had forgotten their responsibilities as parents, she said, and generations of her people had lost their way. That the Mungiki would adopt the mantle of freedom fighters, she added, showed how deeply disconnected young Kikuyus were from their heritage and how twisted and deformed their self-worth and ideas of masculinity had become. Kikuyus weren't alone in this, she suggested; it was simply that their losses were most visible in the history of Kenya both before and after independence.

It didn't only trouble Prof that a proper reckoning of the Mau Mau period had yet to be made; we, the British, had ourselves yet to grasp the nettle of our own responsibility for the trauma of those years. In October 2012, after many years of agitation from British and Kenyan scholars, lawyers, and activists, Britain's High Court finally determined that three elderly Kenyans (Jane Muthoni Mara, Paulo Muoka Nzili, and Wambuga wa Nyingi), who claimed that they'd been tortured by the British authorities during the Mau Mau period, had the right to sue the

British government for damages. The three testified that they'd been, respectively, sexually assaulted, castrated, and beaten unconscious.

As representatives of the many victims of the British regime, these Kenyans wanted to establish a fund for elderly Mau Mau veterans and receive an apology from the British government. In June 2013, the British government agreed to pay £20 million to compensate over five thousand victims of the British colonial administration, although the government insisted that it wasn't legally liable for what the colonial regime had done. Ian Cobain and others writing in *The Guardian* noted that the decision to settle the case followed the discovery of thousands of documents detailing widespread abuse that the U.K.'s foreign office had kept from the public for decades. Only time will tell whether this settlement might lead to further claims for compensation from other victims of the British Empire, as some British historians and politicians fear. Nevertheless, these revelations illustrate that, as Prof herself might put it, the keeping of secrets in the Mau Mau conflict was also not confined to one side.

Although I agree that a case should have been brought by the three Kenyans against the British Government, and although I welcome the possible extension of reparations to all those who were victims of Britain's imperial endeavors, it would be disingenuous of me not to admit that I can hear in my own head the brusque foreshortenings of history found in *Kenya: Britain's Most Attractive Colony* and the familiar tut-tuttings of perpetrators who haven't been held to account—not least by themselves: *It was all so long ago . . . a different era . . . times have changed . . . need to move on.* What Prof taught me is not only how impossible it genuinely is for a people and a society *to move on* without a proper reckoning of the past, but that the past is always prologue to a more damaged and perverse future, if reparation of some sort is withheld, the unspoken claims are not allowed to be voiced, and the broken promises are not in some manner honored. Like the spirit of Waiyaki wa Hinga himself, these issues, although apparently buried, are far from dead.

·   ·   ·

My experience of reading *Love, Life, and Elephants* has obviously been colored by my much closer relationship with and work for Wangari Maathai, and someone reading what I've written so far might conclude that I consider it self-evident that Dame Daphne's personal and social history is blinkered and self-regarding whereas Wangari Maathai's is more genuine and representative of "the ordinary Kenyan's experience," whatever that might mean. Such an assumption would not only be dangerous—laden as it is with everyone's natural desire to be on the right side of history, as it were—but I've found that each layer of the past that I've excavated complicates the one succeeding it, forcing a shift in perspective and rendering any judgments about what we believe to be the proper apportionment of guilt and innocence less and less assured. How much so, I explore in subsequent chapters.

2

Rumi's Elephant

A FAMOUS FABLE that exists in various forms in Muslim, Hindu, Jain, and Buddhist traditions relates how a group of men who are unable to see (they're either blind or in a room without light) are asked to describe an elephant. They each touch a separate part of the animal and, depending on which section of the body their fingers feel, they arrive at very different conclusions as to what an elephant is. This is how the great Sufi poet Jalal al-Din Rumi (1207–1272) tells the story:

> Some Hindus had brought an elephant for exhibition and placed it in a dark house. Crowds of people were going into that dark place to see the beast. Finding that ocular inspection was impossible, each visitor felt it with his palm in the darkness. The palm of one fell

on the trunk. "This creature is like a water-spout," he said.

The hand of another lighted on the elephant's ear. To him the beast was evidently like a fan.

Another rubbed against its leg. "I found the elephant's shape is like a pillar," he said.

Another laid his hand on its back. "Certainly this elephant was like a throne," he said.

Rumi then interprets the story.

The sensual eye is just like the palm of the hand. The palm has not the means of covering the whole of the beast.

The eye of the Sea is one thing and the foam another. Let the foam go, and gaze with the eye of the Sea. Day and night foam-flecks are flung from the sea; oh amazing! You behold the foam but not the Sea. We are like boats dashing together; our eyes are darkened, yet we are in clear water (208).

Wangari Maathai found this fable useful, she once said, because the Green Belt Movement touched people's lives in many different ways—as a tree-planting collective, as a civil-society organization that agitated against corruption and for good governance, as a promoter of peace and reconciliation, as a social-empowerment network for women, as a revenue source for people living in poverty, and as a consciousness-raising institution.

Consequently, Prof said, it was sometimes hard to define exactly what GBM *was*.

Prof wasn't much given to metaphors or similes, at least in English, but she'd occasionally find them useful. In *Unbowed*, she relates how she told a reporter following the 1992 Kenyan elections, when she was a leading member of the opposition, that a female politician needed the skin of an elephant (254). She elaborated on this idea in her chapter in *Speak Truth to Power*, edited by Kerry Kennedy and Eddie Adams. During one of Prof's campaigns, Kenyan politicians had publically ridiculed her: "Parliament was just being mean, chauvinistic, and downright dirty. Fortunately, my skin is thick, like an elephant's. The more they abused and ridiculed me, the more they hardened me. I know I was right, and they were wrong."

That stubbornness and imperviousness to pressure stood Prof in good stead during the difficult years, although these traits could also be frustrating to her friends and colleagues. Decisive and emphatic though she was at times, she also refused to be rushed. When she didn't want to do something, she'd simply stop and become immoveable, even when she'd initiated the project. You might be under the impression that a decision had been reached. However, if you were paying attention, you could usually tell that the conclusion was provisional, that it would need to be reflected upon and its potential outcomes weighed and considered. Sure enough, hours, days, or even months later, the "decision" would be upended. In such moods, one friend commented to me once, Prof could be as intransigent as an elephant.

To stretch the metaphor further, it was my experience that, again proverbially, Prof had an elephantine memory. It wasn't that she had immediate recall or could put a name to every face or vice versa. But her brow would furrow, a quizzical air would spread over her face, and she'd fall silent. Finally, as we chattered around her, she'd bring up a conversation that had occurred many moons previously that contradicted or complicated what was being discussed at the time. You might be frustrated at Prof's resistance to act on something unless she'd mulled it over, but that was the way it was. You never got anything past Prof.

Both Prof and I employ(ed) these tropes, as Prof would say, "with a light touch." But Rumi's story serves a serious purpose. For the Sufi poet, the elephant in the room is a parable that teaches us how easily we're distracted by frothy, superficial appearances (the foam) that caress and dazzle our eyes with their vitality. No matter how attractive the spume is, its insubstantiality diverts us from perceiving what is deeper and more extensive (the Sea), which is all around us and offers us a clear path if we'd only open our inner eye and discern it.

Another message that the tale conveys is that the perceptions we hold of a situation or an individual are reflections not only of the limitations of our experiences but our inherent biases and preconceptions. Although we might be shown a part of the beast that contradicts our belief about what that animal *is*, we still cling to the idea that we've grasped the creature's essence, if only because it was *we* who took the measurements and made the assessments. We see what we want to see, and don't what we don't—especially if our limited perspective runs counter to our expansive narrow-mindedness, as it were. In short, *we* know what an elephant really *is*, because none of us wants to believe that we're as blinkered as everyone else.

How wrong we can be offers a sobering lesson not merely about the relative nature of reality as we perceive it, but just how partial and even willfully mistaken we might be about what we assume is true and real and verifiable. Not only do we think we discern the essence when we only catch a segment, but that segment has the potential to mislead us entirely—affirming only our prejudice and blind spots. Among the many lessons Wangari Maathai taught me, she illustrated this aspect of the elephant for me, too, as this chapter will suggest.

※　　　※　　　※

One Sunday, Mia and I accompanied Prof to a church service in her Tetu constituency, hoping that we might record her either before or after the ceremony, which she advised us mischievously would last perhaps as long as four hours and be conducted entirely in Kikuyu.

The Central Highlands offered a stark contrast to the dry scrub of the districts Mia and I had been driven through as part of the World Neighbors tour. Lush and densely packed acres of bright-green tea and coffee plantations flowed over the countryside—pocked with garden plots, banana bushes, non-indigenous eucalyptus and black wattle trees, and the occasional woodlot of pines standing to regimented attention. Everywhere we looked it seemed, Kenyans were in transit: women lugged huge bundles of sticks on their heads or backs, trucks swerved around the potholes or occasional bicyclist, and every so often we passed families dressed in their dusty Sunday suits and clutching their Bibles. Our driver expertly guided the car along the tarmac, gravel, or compacted mud that carved into the hills. In areas that the Green Belt Movement had yet to cover with non-exotic trees, we frequently saw soil the color of burned terracotta bleeding down gullies into the streams below.

Although Prof had spent more than a decade as a scientist and an academic—indeed, she'd been the first woman in East and Central Africa to receive a doctorate, and had chaired the department of veterinary anatomy at the University of Nairobi—she was deeply engaged with religion and very comfortable in sacred settings. She'd been baptized as a Presbyterian and had converted to Catholicism as a teenager. She was moved by the liturgy and music of Christian worship; while in New York City for medical treatment in the last year of her life, she regularly visited St. Patrick's Cathedral.

As she'd grown older, her views had become more ecumenical. She believed, she said, that many religious traditions directed you toward the divine and that no faith held a monopoly on righteousness. Indeed, so far had she moved that, at times, her views took on a distinctly anti-clerical cast. Aside from the occasional reverential nod to the Vatican and an abiding respect for the nuns who in her eyes had sacrificed so much for her education, Prof held a healthy skepticism toward what one might call the *ekklesia*—particularly as it manifested itself in Kenya. Prof was well aware that the Sunday service broke up the monotony of farming and housework and was a way for the community to come together. She also understood that once you'd reached your destination, something that might take many hours, it was worth making a day of it. Yet she found it unconscionable that church services (of whatever denomination) lasted such a long time and that ordinary men and women would frequently be obliged to walk so far to get to and from the house of worship without being offered anything to eat. She thought it outrageous that services too often descended into a shake-down for the minister's pet project, as ordinary people were pressured into handing over what little money they had to clergy who were happy to expand their coffers but not necessarily their services to the poor.

On our arrival at the church, Mia and I were introduced to the congregation, who expressed what I *think* was their appreciation at our presence, and we settled down for the ceremony to begin. It would have the familiar arc of a Eucharist, except, at a central point in the service, Prof would be invited to speak to the assembly, which she did for about twenty to thirty minutes.

Mia and I had heard Prof speak Kikuyu on the phone and in conversation, but never for such a long time. For me, it was a revelation. Prof was more animated than I'd ever seen her before: gesticulating, leaning forward, her intonation rising and falling in that powerful voice that had grown hoarse after several decades of declamation before large crowds (as well as because, to our continual frustration, she never drank enough water). After the service, we asked Prof what she'd said, and she told us that, as usual, she'd urged people to conserve resources and protect the forests. The fact that, in spite of the occasional English loan word, I had no idea what specifically she was talking about provided me with an admittedly very blurry window through which to observe the various identities she'd adopted over the years.

As she punctuated the air and furrowed her brow, I could detect Wangari the fighter, the woman whom Macharia Kamau, ambassador for the Kenyan mission to the United Nations, called in the 2011 New York City memorial ceremony for Prof, "*Wa-ngari, Wa-ngari*, that powerful matriarchal name of the Kikuyu lineage of warriors, the protectors of Earth and its people." When she'd been beaten about the head in 1998 by security guards hired to prevent her and others from planting trees in Karura Forest, a two-thousand-acre parcel of public land in northern Nairobi, Wangari the warrior had declaimed in English to the media, before going to the police station and signing a report on the attack in her own blood, "We want honesty, we want justice. If we are going to shed blood because of our land, we will. We are used to that. Our forefathers shed blood for land. We will do so. This is my blood. It reminds me of the blood that Waiyaki shed trying to protect Karura Forest."[2]

Waiyaki, of course, was the Kikuyu leader whom the British had tricked in 1890, and the government's allotting of public land to its buddies was yet another act of duplicity in a long line of bad-faith decisions that had enabled those in power to steal the *wananchi*'s property. By evoking Waiyaki, Prof was calling on the warrior spirit that resisted the commodification and privatization of the commons. But Prof that day in 1998 was not only acutely aware of the price that ordinary people—perhaps most especially, I think, *her* ordinary people—had paid for Kenya to become independent, but was also highly sensitive to the location in which she was invoking her battling predecessor. Two generations previously, the Mau Mau rebels had, like the Kikuyu warriors of two generations before them, resisted outside forces by hiding among the trees, behind the waterfalls, and in the caves of the Central Highlands, including those of Karura Forest.

Prof's statement revealed to me that the oaths that Waiyaki made were still relevant for her, although the collaborators and traitors in 1998 may have been different. And it crystallized the sense for me that, although Prof

---

2 Quoted from footage shown in *Taking Root: The Vision of Wangari Maathai*, directed by Lisa Merton and Alan Dater (Marlboro Films, 2008).

may have discussed with us the Mungiki gangs and the psychological dislocation that had affected many Kikuyus, I could never hope genuinely to comprehend how heavily history and the fateful decisions made throughout the century weighed on her and her community. Nor perhaps would I truly fathom the complex and partly compromised relationship that her own family had with the Mau Mau uprising—and to what extent Prof might have had to compensate psychologically to reconcile herself with the push and pull of familial loyalties, and of her father's relationship with Mr. Neylan. That distance wasn't only created because I didn't understand Kikuyu and had no particular feeling for the lived reality of the Kikuyu people, or that 350 years separated me from the civil war that had likewise torn my own country and many families apart. It was that I hadn't had my cultural and spiritual heritage taken from me—either by outsiders or my own kin.

One person who did have some idea of what was at stake was the distinguished paleoanthropologist Louis Leakey, who with his wife Mary unearthed evidence of early human life in Olduvai Gorge in what was then Tanganyika (now Tanzania). Leakey was born in Kibete near Nairobi in 1903 and grew up speaking Kikuyu. In the mid-1930s, he grew concerned that the ancient customs of the Kikuyus were disappearing as many members of the community converted to Christianity and abandoned their cultural practices. Leakey approached a group of elders and asked them whether he might be allowed to write down as much as possible of what they remembered about their rituals, worldview, and knowledge of flora and fauna before they were lost forever.

The elders were initially skeptical. Although Leakey had passed through several of the Kikuyu initiation ceremonies that were required of individuals in their journey from childhood to the varying degrees of elderhood that the society had established, he was not only a foreigner and a white man, but he hadn't attained the degree of initiation that would entitle him to be told all of the history and details of the traditions of the Kikuyu people. Leakey, however, persuaded the elders to reveal to him their secrets through a weighty example. When the Romans had invaded England, he explained to them, the British cultures that were then in existence had been wiped out, and as a result what we knew of them was very limited, or filtered through the lens of those hostile to them. Leakey told the elders that he feared the same might be replicated with the Kikuyus, especially given that their culture was essentially oral in nature.

Prof speculated that the notion that the apparently all-mighty British had themselves undergone cultural destruction would have made a deep impression on the elders. The latter reflected on their recent history and acknowledged that Leakey's observations were correct. In the 1890s, an outbreak of smallpox and a series of retaliatory massacres by white explorers against raids by Kikuyu warriors had severely destabilized the community. We've already seen how white settlers took much of the Kikuyus' most fertile land and introduced a monetized economic and taxation system that forced many Kikuyu men to seek work and land elsewhere. By the mid-1920s, the British colonial administration had banned the Kikuyus' extensive and highly participatory structures of governance—including the *ituika*, the seven-year-long ceremony that served to transfer power from one generation to the next every three decades. Ironically, one of the reasons why the elders initially refused Leakey's request was because his peer-group hadn't been able to go through the *ituika*, which had last been completed in the 1890s. As a result, Leakey and the other Kikuyus his age belonged to a "lost" generation who would never attain power and self-determination.

Once the elders agreed, Leakey undertook an exhaustive series of discussions with those who could recall life prior to his birth and before the arrival of white missionaries and explorers, and the gun, changed Kikuyu life forever. The result of Leakey's interviews and research was *The Southern Kikuyu before 1903*,[3] a three-volume work of ethnography, botany, and cultural archeology that Leakey

---

3 Leakey defined the "Southern Kikuyu" as the population beneath the Chania River which runs to the south of Nyeri township. Leakey indicated that he was obliged to concentrate on the southern Kikuyu, rather than the central or northern Kikuyu as he called them, because there were so many variations in practice that the resulting three volumes would have been considerably longer. Leakey emphasized that although the variations in practice were considerable, the meaning and purpose behind the religious and cultural practices of all three Kikuyu regions remained roughly the same.

compiled in 1937, but which was only edited and published in 1977, some five years after his death.

Prof asked me to read the three volumes of *The Southern Kikuyu before 1903* when we were working on *Replenishing the Earth*, in order to corroborate her personal knowledge and insights on pre-Christian Kikuyuland. I found her observations to be entirely accurate—at least as judged against Leakey's work. In the end, my research and Leakey's biography didn't appear in *Replenishing*, which narrowed in focus to concentrate on the values sustaining the Green Belt Movement. Nonetheless, my reading of Leakey's *magnum opus* and further conversations with Prof enhanced our mutual recognition of the multiple ironies that clustered around Leakey's work . . . and beyond.

The first irony was that Leakey's extraordinary accomplishment and act of cultural conservation was a salvage operation from the decimation caused by the very forces that made *The Southern Kikuyu before 1903* necessary. Leakey had learned Kikuyu because his parents were Christian missionaries who'd come to Africa to evangelize. The funding for his research came from the trust set up by arch-imperialist Cecil Rhodes (1853–1902), not known for his sensitivity to non-white ethnicities or belief in cultural relativism. Moreover, Leakey's motivations, Prof suggested, were not entirely above suspicion. In spite of his admiration for Kikuyu culture and his warnings about what effect colonialism might have on the local peoples of East Africa, he was still eager to curry favor with the

British colonial administration in order to access archeo-logical sites.

Prof wondered aloud to me whether the elders had been initially reluctant to grant interviews to a man who in many ways had grown up with the Kikuyu because of the empty promises that the perfidious Captain Lugard and other British authorities had made to them from the 1890s onward. Was these elders' doubt about Leakey and the written word itself a response to how lightly the Brit-ish took the oral vows that had been made? And, beyond that, given what had occurred to the community follow-ing Waiyaki's betrayal, could one trust *any* white man—no matter how well-intentioned or embedded he was within the micro-nation—to report the truth and use it for the good of the people and not for his own advantage?

Prof observed that the fact that she knew *The South-ern Kikuyu before 1903*, rather than any putative title that might have been produced by the men whose knowl-edge the paleoanthropologist unearthed to memorialize the past of her own community, was another paradoxical burden that literate cultures imposed on oral ones. She found it tragic and absurd that Africans often had to visit European museums to see artifacts from their own culture. It was, she considered, yet another sad reflection of how dependent Africans were on the willingness of foreigners to value and evaluate, catalogue and archive, their cultural artifacts—even as they were disappearing from the conti-nent, often at the same hands. Prof remarked astringently that in order to understand the history of her own people, she had to read English, the mode of learning and language that from the outset defined and separated Kikuyus who were "modern" from those who even her own people would soon come to consider primitive.

Prof was acutely conscious of the fact that her command of English and exposure to the larger English-speaking world had allowed her to rise from a humble background, enter the very small group of elite black men and women in Kenya in the 1960s, and thence to ascend to a platform whereby she could address a much wider audience than she would have been able to had the colonial school system not provided her with such an education.

Even so, she reminded Mia and me on several occasions that neither English nor Kiswahili was her first language, and that they were each in their way foreign impositions on cultures that already had their own identities and tongues. English and Kiswahili were not only passports to wider communication but also tools of oppression—one of the colonial powers, the other a composite of local dialects and that of the Arab slave-traders. For the ordinary citizen, who might not understand or speak English at all and know Kiswahili only haltingly, the promises of a politician in either language were, literally, meaningless. How could you hold someone to account when you had no idea what they were talking about? In fact, Prof says in *Challenge*, to this day the African elites depend on keeping their citizens ignorant so they can get away with aggregating to themselves the country's present and future treasure.

This ambivalence extended to micro-national identity

itself. As proud as Prof was of her heritage and the central role that Kikuyus had played in the struggle for independence, she was intensely conscious that over-identification with one's ethnic group had resulted in political and social turmoil in Kenya and especially in other micro-nationalities' resentment of, and distrust toward, Kikuyus, who constituted the largest ethnic group in Kenya. The founding president, Jomo Kenyatta, whose 1938 book *Facing Mt. Kenya* had for years provided the sole insider's anthropological examination of Kikuyu culture, was one, as was Mwai Kibaki, the nation's third president. He left office in 2013, to be replaced by another Kikuyu: Jomo's son, Uhuru.

Prof knew very well how much mischief micro-nationalism could cause. In the early 1980s, she was accused of championing the cause of GEMA (an association of Gikuyus, Embu, and Merus), which according to its enemies fostered interethnic rivalry, and as an economic and political bloc sought to dominate Kenyan public life. When during the course of the writing of *Unbowed* we asked Prof whether GEMA was an organization for ethnic chauvinists, Prof dismissed the notion. She mentioned, without irony, that accusing political foes of stirring up ethnic conflict was a tactic often used by supporters of Daniel arap Moi, who was a member of the Kalenjin cluster of micro-nationalities. She argued that Moi's insistence on a national identity that transcended ethnic background was disingenuous, and that, come election time, he and other politicians used resentment at the visibility and perceived dominance of Kikuyus to retain hold on power.

Prof's reply to me about GEMA was no doubt true; but whether it was the only truth, I couldn't say. She was utterly opposed to violence and loathed the use of ethnocentrism to score political advantage. However, I always wondered whether there wasn't a part of Prof that was aggrieved at the disproportionate price the Kikuyus had paid to achieve independence for Kenya, and that that feeling hadn't in some way influenced her worldview. How could it not have? Wherever the balance might have lain in these narratives, either Wangari the warrior wasn't going to tell us or, like the metaphor of the elephant in the room, no individual paragraph or episode was going to reveal the whole story.

*   *   *

As Prof addressed the congregation in the church that Sunday, her voice both cajoled and insisted; her brow creased, and she smiled and laughed. The congregation would respond in kind, their voices exhaling the sound that for me became synonymous with the Kikuyu language: an extended *hay* with a silent *h*. It seemed to mean everything from "I understand what you're saying," to "I'm not sure about that," to "Tell me about it!" to "I hear you, my friend!" It acted as a verbal *punkt*—the equivalent of *hmm*, the French *donc*, or the Turkish *şey*, perhaps. It was an antiphon and an echo, an almost continual murmur whose breathiness was the essence of aspiration and inspiration, exasperation and dissent.

Prof continued to work the assembly, and another Maathai emerged: Wangari the politician, attempting to persuade people of her view. For all her qualms about the Church demanding too much of its parishioners and her dislike of politics delivered from the pulpit, Prof knew it was useful to take part in this service because it allowed her to reach a large number of constituents simultaneously in one location rather than burn up valuable hours, gasoline, and a vehicle's shock absorbers negotiating the slopes and hairpin bends of the Central Highlands. In turn, the parishioners expected to be addressed and informed by their Member of Parliament, and Prof freely used biblical stories and motifs to communicate her message. The missionaries had done their work well, Prof would comment. Everyone, no matter how unlettered or provincial, knew the Bible. It was for her the *lingua franca* for conversation about, or conversion to, conservation.

Strange to say, in spite of Prof's formidable rhetorical gifts—she almost always spoke extemporaneously and at length—I'm not sure she was particularly successful as a politician, and not only because she failed to win an election three times. She knew the theatrics that the media love and was adept at using them. Once roused to action she exhibited great personal determination in seeing a situation through to the end. For all her personal magnetism, however, she often struck me as cautious and reactive, unwilling or perhaps unable to exploit a situation to her immediate political advantage. These are in many ways admirable traits, but they didn't necessarily help her in her attempt to woo voters.

As she exhorted the parishioners that day in church, I took some of the facial gestures of her audience and a certain shuffling in the pews as hints that not everything she said was being greeted with complete approval. In other forums, we heard both from her and others close to her that her constituents weren't happy that she still criticized the government of which she was a member and that she didn't show enough support for the president, whose constituency bordered hers. For all her support of micro-national pride, an aggravation for her and other Kenyans was that political parties in her country were organized along ethnic rather than ideological lines. You voted for a party because it looked after the narrow interests of your people rather than because you held conservative or liberal economic or social positions. Once in power, your party was not expected to enact a policy program so much as to deliver the state's wealth to the ethnic group it represented. Once a micro-nationality gained power it was now, as the saying went, their "time to eat."

Prof found this attitude infuriating, as she did the notion of a Member of Parliament using his or her salary as a public purse for constituents. As we waited outside her parliamentary office in Nairobi or joined her in her constituency, we observed a steady stream of supplicants asking if she might be able to help with hospital fees, funeral costs, or money for school supplies or a uniform. The MP, Prof would explain, was expected to do this because their job had made them rich. She felt sorry for the people who showed up in her office or came to her cap in hand when she was visiting her constituency. They were so poor and desperate, she said, and it made her very sad that they couldn't meet the expenses for even the most elementary of life's demands. It would, she added, have been heartless to turn them down. Yet it was, she knew, a vision of public service that only exacerbated dishonesty and encouraged unscrupulous fortune hunters, who doled out money to persuade people to vote for them and then showered cash on friends and relatives following the election.

Prof was immensely proud of the mechanisms she and other MPs established to allow local communities to decide how state revenue was spent, rather than continue the top–down delivery of money that fostered dishonesty in the form of, say, ad-hoc sweeteners to a local chief for his son's schooling or to pay for a cousin's funeral. But the old ways of doing business die hard, and it's my guess that Prof lost the 2007 election to a more pliant candidate because she refused to dish out enough cash to the "right" people as much as her perceived disloyalty to the (Kikuyu) president or the international matters that took time away from constituency affairs.

Although we and other supporters were disappointed that Prof never became Kenya's (and Africa's) first female president, despite a run for the office in 1997, she had good reason to remain cautious about fully embracing the political life. The country, she reasoned (incorrectly), wouldn't accept yet another Kikuyu in the highest office, and she couldn't very well campaign against the current president. It was also a fact that Kenya's array of security and paramilitary forces had a nasty habit of ending the lives of those whom their political masters considered a threat to the status quo. This meant you had to be careful about how far you were willing to stick your neck out lest it be cut off.

Here, too, Mia and I, comfortably ensconced in states with a history of respecting freedom of assembly and speech, had little grasp of just how dangerous it was to protest against a regime. Prof would tell us how she'd been forced into hiding or had had to escape overseas for a time (a convenient international conference would provide her with some respite) when the situation became too "hot" in Kenya. She recalled for us the trepidation she'd felt driving past groups of young men by the roadside dressed as traditional warriors and carrying weapons during the so-called tribal clashes in the Rift Valley in the 1990s. In 1993, under threat of arrest, torture, or worse, Prof had been compelled to disguise her appearance and hide behind the front seats of friends' cars as they sped through the Nairobi night from safe house to safe house.

Over and over again in the course of working on her books, we'd respond to these and other stories by asking her for more detail about what happened and what her exact emotions were. She complied as much as she felt comfortable with, but there was an intangible, studied vagueness about her descriptions of such incidents and what she felt. She'd name somebody who'd caused her grief when she'd been in opposition, only to change the accused to the more generic "elements in the government" in a later draft—opting, like Daphne Sheldrick in her memoir, to use the passive voice and a broad statement rather than apportion direct blame. The circumlocution was no doubt a recognition that the Kenyan elite was still sufficiently few in number that she'd likely have to do business with those whom she might condemn in print, and it was therefore safer and more strategic not to name them at all. Following the politicized ethnic violence that occurred after the 2007 elections, Prof made it clear to us that even some of those whom she counted as allies had blood on their hands. It was at once shrewd tactics and life-preserving tact that made it essential sometimes to withdraw and wait rather than sally forth and act.

In its place another, contrarian persona presented itself to the public: Wangari the prophet. She would take on the worn and unwelcome mantle of seers of yore and become the gadfly stinging the complacent body politic. She was the ignored and even despised voice crying in the wilderness against those who'd gone astray, the hectoring irritant of those in power. This particular Wangari refused to toe party lines and accept a status quo that, in her eyes, harmed the environment and forfeited the future of her country. She was the conscience of the nation who used any dais or podium as a pulpit to preach the virtues of self-reliance, public service, honesty, and a commitment to the environment—as she did that Sunday in church.

In contrast to Prof the politician—who veered rhetorically between bold and direct confrontation with authorities that abused their power and a tone of bemused, even offended bafflement at why any individual gifted with intelligence and the opportunities afforded by their education to assume positions of authority would lie and cheat—Prof the prophet insisted that she hadn't felt fear when she was faced with personal danger; nor did she think of herself as particularly courageous. She'd been motivated simply by something being wrong; someone had asked her for help and she'd responded; it was inconceivable that wrong should be allowed to prevail. These principles, she said, had been enough for her to move.

For all the honors she gained abroad, Wangari the prophet occasionally appeared out of sync with the people in the pews and around the country. They clearly admired her; they felt that she belonged to them. But as her speech continued that morning, I sensed a certain fatigue shaping their responses, and not because she was speaking at length. One of Prof's constant laments to us was that Kenyans from every walk of life and level of society had lost the values necessary for lasting economic, social, and environmental renewal. She hated that, as she perceived it, whether in the highest echelons of government or the most economically deprived communities, citizens were more concerned with their own immediate material gain than planning for long-term, sustainable progress.

At times, I'm sure, Prof came across to her fellow citizens as an annoying scold, constantly telling people not to clear the public forests where the soil was good to grow crops (the *shamba* system), but to leave the trees alone and conserve them for the future. For some of these people, who had little problem with the system and were recipients of what I imagine were fairly frequent tongue-lashings, Prof's national and international profile may have been a source of pride. However, that very visibility must have paradoxically made her not only seem remote in office in the way that the pre-Nobel, opposition figure hadn't been, but in their eyes rendered her a rigid, even doctrinaire disciplinarian without the moral and political flexibility that they'd come to expect from a Member of Parliament.

It's possible that the relentlessness of Wangari Maathai was, as is the way with prophets, not only out of temper with her people but also the times she lived in. Although she recognized the power of market forces to bring about rapid change in society (for both good and ill), she was adamant that values and leadership were essential if any nation was to flourish. In some way, these virtues (a commitment to public service, honesty, love of the natural world, and self-determination) felt old-fashioned: holdovers from the 1960s and the early, heady days of independence; outmoded for a world that championed open markets and free trade, micro-credit and philanthrocapitalism, and where a young, burgeoning, and very busy African middle class aspired to consumer goods and social mobility.

When we asked Prof what she thought about the development of robust institutions as a means to check power, so that even a bad leader couldn't do too much harm, Prof insisted on returning to the indispensability of leadership and honest visionaries, such as Julius Nyerere of Tanzania and Nelson Mandela of South Africa, who dedicated themselves to the welfare of the people rather than their own self-aggrandizement and enrichment. For Prof, it wasn't enough for the state to constrain the powerful because all power corrupts; the powerful had to be intrinsically good if the country was to succeed.

*   *   *

Prof the warrior, politician, and prophet were only three sides of this multifaceted, fascinating woman—including *personae* that reflected what the world wanted to see as much as, if not more than, what she wished to present. To my frustration, some of the Western media played down Prof's activism on behalf of a vibrant civil society in favor of a profile that came close to that of the "traditionally built" Botswanan Mma Ramotswe (the spunky and genial heroine of Alexander McCall Smith's *No. 1 Ladies' Detective Agency*), who sees that justice is done and wrongs are righted but in a way that doesn't threaten the political or social order. She was Wangari with the radiant smile, the infectious laugh, and the cheerful disposition, who planted trees, loved children, hugged everyone, and told stories about a hummingbird, a fig tree, and frogs' eggs. Or she became a sort of Earth Mother, elementally connected to the land and effusing a free-good and fuzzy spirituality with which native or non-Western peoples are frequently and lazily endowed in the Euro-American imagination. Or she embodied a reassuring and infinitely forgiving womanhood that both flirted with a Mammy stereotype and, ironically, matched the femininity that her (male) political opponents in Kenya would have preferred her to express when they complained that she wasn't traditional enough an African woman.

On occasion, she used the preconceptions of Africa in the West quite deliberately. She told us that she felt a certain responsibility to be the inspirational Wangari who represented a compelling contrast with the image of the continent south of the Sahara that for too long had been depicted (at its best) as a continent full of charismatic megafauna, baking sun, impenetrable forests or endless plains, and happy, dancing natives; and (at its worst) as a benighted landmass populated by absurd dictators and children with distended bellies, both holding Kalashnikovs—an Africa at once exotic and mysterious or an ungovernable and incomprehensible mess of warring factions and endemic poverty.

I think she relished being Wangari the doer, no-nonsense and practical. As opposed to the egomaniacal, fat-bellied, and thin-skinned Big Men in their dark glasses—so deliciously and uproariously satirized in Ngugi wa Thiong'o's Rabelaisian epic *Wizard of the Crow*—who sat behind the tinted windows of their Mercedes Benzes, flanked by motorcycle outriders and surrounded by an over-staffed security detail, Prof was the non-governmental organizer who, even as a government minister, only traveled with one bodyguard and a driver; who honored rather than abandoned her rural roots when education catapulted her into the elite; and who worked alongside women, showing how solution-oriented, collective purpose could bring about meaningful change.

She cannily knew when to employ Wangari the good Catholic schoolgirl to defuse dangerous situations or destabilize opponents. She'd be deferential to authority and protocol, only speak when spoken to, and answer the question she was asked rather than grandstand or stick to her talking points. She'd always want a story or a paragraph to have a moral, and when in trouble would state (with a delicate mix of puzzlement and archness) that, in effect, all little old Wangari was doing was planting trees and not fomenting rebellion. And she was "Prof," the lecturer and esteemed academic, the woman concerned with science and pedagogy: the teacher of us all.

Prof's ability to use her various masks when she needed them—navigating her way through the turbulent and treacherous political currents of post-independence Kenya—hints at a struggle familiar to many colonized peoples: the balancing of the *personae* imposed upon one by colonial and post-colonial ethnic, state, and regional identities with those one dons oneself both as an act of resistance and a declaration of the self.

Prof showcased this psychomachia in the most literal form of her identification. Her Kikuyu name, the one given to her by her parents, was Wangari Muta. At her baptism as a child, Miriam became her Christian name, and Wangari her last, and Muta was dropped. When she converted to Catholicism as a teenager, she was supplied with yet another name: Mary Josephine, or Mary Jo. Thus, it was as Mary Josephine Wangari that she received a scholarship to study at the Benedictine college of Mount St. Scholastica in Atchison, Kansas, in 1960.

Inspired by the African states that were becoming independent in the early 1960s and the simultaneous movement for civil rights in the United States, Prof began to reclaim her African heritage. She wrote her name as Mary Josephine Wangari Muta, and then reversed the first names, becoming Wangari Mary Josephine Muta. By the time she arrived back in Kenya in 1966, she'd come full circle to the name she'd had at birth: Wangari Muta. When she married her husband, Mwangi Mathai, she took his name (reluctantly, because it was a British custom and not indigenous), only to add a second "a" following her divorce, to emphasize the pronunciation of "Māthai" and, I fancy, to differentiate herself from him. In that way, she became Wangari Muta Maathai.

*   *   *

How complex and contested this space can be—a struggle between self-definition and others' ideas about one and the various narratives one tells and hears about one's identity—is encapsulated for me by a story that broke shortly after Prof was awarded the Nobel and morphed into Wangari Maathai, the international celebrity. In reporting the honor, *The Economist* magazine wrote on October 14, 2004 (quoting a journalist's record of words that Prof had reportedly said at a recent rally), that Prof had "controversial ideas about AIDS":

> She thinks the virus was created by "evil-minded scientists" to kill blacks: "It is created by a scientist for biological warfare." Ms Maathai also argues that condoms cannot prevent transmission of the virus. Coming from one of the first women in east Africa to earn a doctorate, Ms Maathai's views might be seen as surprising. Coming from a freshly crowned Nobel laureate, they might be considered inexcusable.

Prof issued a statement that the original report had misquoted her. She said that she'd been responding to what people in her constituency, and not she herself, thought about the virus and how it was created. As an MP, she indicated, she'd worked hard to raise awareness and remove the stigma of HIV/AIDS, and to provide screening and nutritional services for those with the disease.

What interested me about *The Economist*'s outrage was how snugly such a view fit within several of the *personae* identified in this chapter. These "characters" presented convenient *mythoi* that might not offer a consistent vision but satisfied a number of narratives about Africa that the West remains invested in.

One narrative reminded us that despite the education

that gifted, intelligent, and talented individuals from the colonies may have received from the West and the former colonial powers, they were essentially radicals, which meant they bore an animus toward the white man and to Civilization, Science, and Progress. It was a narrative that reminded us that Nelson Mandela co-founded the *armed* wing of the African National Congress and embraced Muammar Qaddafi and Fidel Castro; and that Thabo Mbeki, Mandela's successor as president of South Africa, held non-scientific attitudes about the origin and treatment of AIDS that delayed the general availability of anti-retroviral drugs in his country. It echoed the century-old story of how an African presented one face to the white man and another to his fellow Africans: whether he was the Mau Mau apologist and untrustworthy Kikuyu nationalist, supportive of secret oathings, superstitions, and unspeakable rites; or subservient and genial one moment and subversive and vicious the next; or an African from whom the veneer of civilization was easily removed to reveal the primitive beneath.

Another narrative, the kind offered by those critical of how Africa had become overly dependent on foreign aid, would affirm that, yes, Wangari Maathai *was* a radical. Her message of self-reliance and her contempt for the culture of dependency undercut Western hegemony and international aid agencies, which in collusion with crooked African client states kept ordinary people from determining their own future. By arguing for the revitalization of local cultures and practices, she was questioning the validity and viability of the post-independence state, and arguing for a return to the wisdom of indigenous African healers and leadership. In her utilization of the conspiracy theory, this line of thinking would run, Prof was simply asking ordinary people to think critically about all received wisdom from centralized authorities (whether colonial or post-colonial), especially when the powerful had so poorly served the powerless.

Yet another narrative is one not so easily contained within the pithy condemnations of *The Economist* or the praise of those who wanted Prof to be the revolutionary darling of post-colonial subaltern activism. Although she employed the language and actions associated with the political left—fighting the oppressive powers that be, working at the grassroots, inherently communitarian in her organization of the disenfranchised rural poor—she was, in many ways, a conservative. As much as she was skeptical of corporate "greenwashing," she welcomed the support of businesses that she felt were genuinely committed to preserving the environment. She spoke out forcefully for the conservation of biodiversity, yet she was non-committal in the debate over whether genetically modified crops were potentially dangerous environmental pollutants or offered an opportunity for farmers to increase their yields.

She was a champion of the rule of law and human rights, yet she was careful to speak of "democratic space" as opposed to "democracy," partly because she felt that good governance could take many forms, as long as the leaders had integrity and presented a positive and sustainable vision for their country. For all her desire to effect change within parliament, she nevertheless honored self-discipline, virtue, character, and service based on a higher calling, qualities that didn't necessitate governmental action or money to cultivate. Corruption was not, for her, a preserve only of the rich and powerful; the poor were often their own worst enemies.

The Civic and Environmental Education seminars that she organized for *wananchi* were not merely about identifying bad governance and raising consciousness among the disadvantaged, but forums where communities were encouraged to recognize how their *own* behavior and decisions had either brought about or aggravated their situation and powerlessness. She wanted ordinary individuals—no matter how exploited they might be— to recognize their own agency in locating a problem and solving it. It was, she would sigh, hard work. As she would often lament, "the bottom is heavy": those with the fewest resources in society made any effort to uplift them that much more difficult by failing to help themselves and to maximize the opportunities that others provided them with.

This ambiguity extended to gender relations. Yes, she loved to tell stories about how she and other women had bested male authorities and was both baffled and angered by the abuse and contempt that men heaped on her and other women. Yet she resisted calling herself a "feminist," partly, I think, because it conjured an image in her mind of a confrontational attitude that felt too "Western" to her, or as the Kenyan professor Namulandah Florence has suggested, to many African women. Although she challenged gender stereotypes in the public sphere, argues Florence, Prof remained quite conservative regarding gender relations in the domestic sphere. When Mia and I called the Green Belt Movement *a woman's organization*, a nomenclature that Prof herself had played off throughout her career as a public figure and which she accepted as an identity in the public's mind, she'd observe that it didn't matter whether you were a man without shoes or a woman walking barefoot: both of you were equally unshod and both had a part to play in GBM.

To that extent, she wasn't a partisan or ideologue; she was uncomfortable with a politics that might box her in or force her to adopt positions that she wasn't completely sure of. She resisted a systematic political philosophy, which meant that, at times, she contradicted herself. For instance, I'm not sure she ever reconciled her wish for a more functional state that protected minority rights and the environment (one, like Nyerere's Tanzania, that was very centralized and where the learning of Kiswahili was compulsory) with a strengthened sense of micro-national identity (partially as a response to the predatory state) that might lead to a resurgence of ethnic chauvinism. Nor, despite her oft-stated concern about the burdens that the poor imposed upon those who were trying to help them out, do I think she ever worked out how far the obligations of elites extended toward them without reinforcing the very dependency and lack of initiative she decried. For all her wish to encourage self-motivation in others, Prof liked to be in charge.

Mia and I didn't shy away from asking Prof to reconcile cultural norms with contemporary "civilized" behavior, as *The Economist* was suggesting she'd failed to do. During the course of our work on *The Challenge for Africa*, we asked her to comment on stories in the news such as communities accusing its members of witchcraft and the murder of albinos in Tanzania. We wanted to know what she thought about the continuing practice of female circumcision (also called "female genital mutilation" or FGM) in some societies in Africa.

Prof's response was finely calibrated. She pointed out that many Africans had experienced enormous stresses in their lives. Some civil wars had lasted decades, leading to generational trauma and long-term displacement from homes, communities, and livelihoods. People frequently lost loved ones to treatable diseases such as malaria as well as AIDS. All these conditions had been exacerbated by the systemic failure of state agencies to protect the people or relieve them of suffering; in fact, she noted, the state may itself have been complicit in creating the lack of security.

Given the breakdown of the traditional cultures that would have furnished ordinary people with some kind of defense to cope with loss and change, these individuals scrambled for an answer as to why events occurred that seemed incomprehensible—visited on them by forces and from regions they had no knowledge of or means to evaluate or respond to. Sometimes, she noted, this lack of critical apparatus to judge one's life situation expressed itself in fervor for the sanctioned religious practices of Christianity and Islam—whether the promises of material wealth held by "prosperity theology" or the clarifying, organizing attractions of fundamentalism. Other times, it directed its attention to scapegoating those who appeared different or centered on a conspiracy from an "outside," malevolent force that had secret powers (such as an evil scientist or an albino or a witch). On still other occasions, it manifested itself in clinging to old ways of expressing a cultural identity—ways that didn't serve that community in the form they'd done before, but instead weakened and marginalized that society, even as they provided the illusion of strength and pride. Perhaps, she observed, this was why practices such as genital cutting, or putting on the war paint and taking out the machetes and bows and arrows to assert oneself following an election, still persisted.

She acknowledged that the Kikuyus had practiced FGM and polygamy until relatively recently. She didn't agree with these customs, she added, but they obviously held some purpose within the community. Polygamy and a patriarchy of the kind that had been practiced by her father, she observed, at least gave families a degree of stability and allowed widows and otherwise unattached children to be looked after and cared for, as opposed to being abandoned to prostitution or sniffing glue on the streets of Nairobi and Mombasa. She was in no doubt that, had the British colonial forces not interrupted the *ituika*, the ritual handing over of power to the next generation, her micro-nationality would have been compelled to examine their rituals and worldview and work their relationship out with modernity. Over time, she averred, they would have sloughed off the old ways and adopted new ones, without the fragmentation and loss of self-confidence that had occurred.

Mia and I might have hoped for a more rigorous rejection, but Prof wasn't going to give it. She was a moralist and a provocateur, whose many *personae* challenged expectations and conventions and forced one to think. She demanded people question their assumptions about the part of the elephant they were touching. She encouraged those who came into contact with her ideas to ask themselves whether they—whatever cultural or intellectual background they claimed—really were more advanced, more sophisticated, more capable of responding reasonably, accurately, proportionally, objectively, or responsibly to the world and what it threw our way than those in the past or in other parts of the world.

I took Prof at her word when she said she didn't think AIDS was created in a lab. I can see how evoking such a story might have allowed a community to comfort itself with its own victimization, and how, by echoing it to reject it, Prof might have been forcing the community to change that identity to something with more agency and less fear. But what if she had said and did believe what *The Economist* reported? Would it really have changed my feelings for her?

Almost certainly not. As I write, a report claims that

fully sixty percent of Republicans in the United States still believe that Barack Obama was not born in the country of which he is president. The Internet is filled with rumors that shadowy forces connected to the government staged or faked the massacre of twenty young children in Newtown, Connecticut, in December 2012 to force people to give up their guns, or planted the bombs at the finish line to the Boston Marathon in April 2013. Serious and intelligent people continue to argue that thousands of people died on September 11, 2001, in New York, Washington, and Pennsylvania due to an elaborate conspiracy cooked up by the U.S. or another government. Theories about how the Bankers, the Jews, the United Nations, the Vatican, the Illuminati, or some other shadowy and unknowable cabal of Chosen Ones *really* rule the world have proved tenaciously seductive within Western societies for centuries.

Each conspiracy produces vast amounts of "evidence" to support its case—claimed to be every bit as "scientific" and "irrefutable" as the rigors demanded by post-Enlightenment skepticism and the *bien-pensant* readers of *The Economist*, myself among them. All such revelations remind me of how blind we are to our own predilections, and how in order to cope with trauma or information that runs counter to our most deeply held views of the world we would rather construct "facts" that bolster our sense of what *should* be true than adjust our perspectives to those facts that *may* be true. We all hold fast to our part of the elephant. Why should Wangari Maathai be any different?

Or, for that matter, me. As I worked with Prof on her books, I'd ask her questions and she dutifully addressed them. Out of these responses, I'd generate manuscripts that I'd read aloud and she would comment on further, before ultimately going over the texts herself on the computer or in long-hand. I would read relevant books, websites, and newspapers, and buttress her arguments with data. From time to time, I wondered to myself whether I should do more research, interview more people, press Prof more on the tough issues: What did she think about gay rights, for instance, or bride price, or body scarification rituals? What about her marriage or her role as a mother? Did I have some kind of responsibility to an abstract Truth in representing her to the world?

But I wasn't a journalist or investigative reporter; I'd been hired to work for *her*, and when she told me, for instance, that she didn't want to risk embroiling her family publically as they had been when her marriage ended, I took that as a decision not to ask or say any more. Prof told the tales she wanted, with all of the candor, lacunae, and evasions by which all of us organize and narrate the story of our lives. And like any of us as we spin our yarns, some of Prof's long-cherished anecdotes or parables probably grew in the telling, embroidered and elaborated in a manner that public speakers who know which parts work and those which don't would be familiar with. Perhaps that's what happened that day when she was "misquoted"—that a good story got out of hand and was overheard by an audience much bigger than the one she was addressing.

Perhaps what she said immediately on hearing the news of her receipt of the Nobel Peace Prize held true that day: "I didn't know anyone was listening."

In the course of our work on her books, Prof resisted the idea that we talk to others: "Let them write their own book," she'd say. Prof did allow us to speak to the taciturn Dr. Makanga, her companion at our first meeting in Kenya in 2001. Inevitably perhaps, the good doctor wryly informed us that he would tell us fifty-two percent of the truth. It would be up to us, lay the playful suggestion, to work out just which was which. Some would find such constraints insupportable or risible, harrumph that it was our duty to get to the essence of the real Wangari Maathai: to find Rumi's infinitely supporting Sea beneath the froth. I don't doubt that Prof was honest with us, even though she didn't tell us everything. But would it have been so "untrue"—or not have suited both Prof *and* us—if she hadn't like Dr. Makanga also kept half of herself uncanny and private, while I and readers could satisfy ourselves that we'd touched the more representative parts of the elephant?

*   *   *

As this chapter has explored, Rumi's pachyderm is subject to the numerous prejudices and projections of the identities that we blind men wish to impose upon it. However, it's worth pointing out at this stage of the excavation another metaphorical elephant in the room: an imposing reality that one may have wished to ignore but can't.

Throughout this book I've chosen the honorific *Prof* because of my perhaps overly punctilious belief that calling her *Wangari*, which is how I generally addressed her in person and think of her, feels too intimate, almost intrusive, not merely on my behalf but on yours, the reader's—as if the process of writing and reading this book allowed us to collude and pretend that we knew her well. That reticence isn't coyness on my part. It's simply a recognition that, some seventy years after Louis Leakey had attempted to gather for posterity material from the Kikuyu elders, I—another uprooted Briton, and, in my case, the great-grandson of an Anglican priest and scholar—was asking this particular Kikuyu elder to do the same.

How could there not hang in the air questions of trust, betrayal, and the advancement of one's own interests at the expense of another? I'd like to believe that I didn't break my promise to her (as she didn't to us), and that what you're reading is an honest and affectionate accounting of a remarkable period in our lives. But, as we know, the feel, shape, and texture of a story, like the elephant, can appear very different to one person than they do to another.

A telling instance of how intricate our connection could be and what was at stake for Prof occurred one evening at the Fairview Hotel, which was conveniently located near her office at the ministry of the environment in Nairobi. We were still at an early stage of recording following the award of the Nobel. Prof, wrapped in her blue shawl against the chill, was uncharacteristically subdued as she related to us how her uncle Thumbi had been forced to join the British armed forces at the outbreak of World War I. (The story appears on pages 27 and 28 of the American edition of *Unbowed*.)

Thumbi's mother, Prof's paternal grandmother, advised her son, who was then no more than twenty years old, to hide from the authorities behind a waterfall near Ihithe. His mother brought him food. He was not safe for long. "[T]he British had developed a system to deal with parents who were reluctant to give up their sons to the war effort," Prof writes. "They would confiscate all of their livestock. For people at that time, especially men, livestock was everything, as important as land. The authorities confronted my grandfather and threatened to take all his cattle and goats. The pressure worked. He told them where his son was hiding and they went and seized him."

Prof's grandfather was sure his son would return, but his wife was equally certain he wouldn't. Prof's grandmother was correct, and Thumbi became one of the more than 100,000 Kikuyus who died during the war, fighting the Germans and Italians in what was then German East Africa (modern-day Tanzania) or from disease shortly after the war ended. The grandparents never discovered their son's fate until much later, when a man informed them that he'd seen Thumbi shot on the battlefield. "My grandmother cried for her son for the rest of her life," Prof added, "and she always blamed my grandfather for the loss. 'I told you he wouldn't come back,' she would say."

Prof had known something was amiss in the family tree and had asked her mother why her uncles and aunt were naming their children after her father. "In Kikuyu culture," Prof said, "traditionally the first son is named for his paternal grandfather, so I always thought my father was my grandparents' eldest son. Later, I learned that my father was named after my grandmother's father, so there must have been another son. In explaining this, my mother told me that my grandmother had been so distraught at what happened to her son that she decided that none of her grandchildren would be named for him, lest she be reminded of that loss. The name of that young man—my eldest uncle—was lost with him, wiped from the face of the earth.

"My grandparents and other families like them who lost sons in World War I never received any official word about what had happened to their children, or any compensation," Prof continued. "This is still an open wound. I want to say to the British government, 'My uncle went to war and never came back, and nobody ever bothered to come and tell my grandparents what had happened to their son.'"

Prof finished and we fell silent. She was almost completely shrouded in darkness, the glow of her skin reflected dimly in the lights scattered throughout the Fairview's lush grounds. The air seemed to thicken around us and my heart sank. I felt compelled to speak, to utter something that acknowledged that I as an Englishman was in some way connected to what had happened to Uncle Thumbi. I told her I was sorry.

Prof waved a hand in my direction and muttered that it didn't matter—her face registering neither approval nor disapproval at my apology. I immediately regretted what I'd done. Prof knew I wasn't personally to blame: no one from my family had threatened Prof's grandparents, or had forced Thumbi to join the army, or had failed to inform his parents of whether or how their son had died. Yet, all good intentions aside, any words I might offer were importunate, self-serving, even petty and ignoble—an irritant rather than a salve for the "open wound" that she and thousands of other families continued to suffer from. In an echo of the case brought before the High Court by the three victims of the Mau Mau struggle, the personal lament only drew attention to the decades-long silence of the British government. For Prof and the three complainants, these abuses needed not a private recognition of a public grief, but the reverse.

Neither my apology nor any response from Prof would remove the duplicity and sordidness of blackmail, or the anger that Thumbi's mother must have felt at her husband's naivety and his blithe assurance that their son would live. More pointedly, it wouldn't alter the fact that, because of the Kikuyu naming customs, not only Thumbi himself but an entire line of the extended family had been eradicated. It was if Thumbi's life and death were a black hole. One was only aware of his presence because the light of that family had been warped as it bent around the impenetrable, unspeakable, and literally unnamable sorrow of his absence. Or, to put it another way, a branch of the family tree had simply withered to a stump, leaving the trunk forever misshapen.

Prof's recollection of what happened to her uncle was one of several instances where I realized that, for all of what I took to be our rapport—the pleasure and inspiration I received from her company, the jokes I told that made her laugh, my boundless respect for her insights, my deeply held wish to do the right thing by her, and her oft-stated gratitude for Mia and my work with and support of her, her family, and the Green Belt Movement—something would always be withheld. And not only that, but that it might *need* to be, if a portion of her self, unarticulated but maybe deeper, truer, even fundamental, was to survive: Prof's own version of the sea beneath the froth. It hinted that the silence of Dr. Makanga and his playing of the percentages might not have been natural taciturnity or harmless waggery, but a strategic decision to maintain some degree of self-determination in the face of these *wazungu* wanting to tell "*the* African story" one more time.

3

The Dreams of Men . . .

WANGARI MAATHAI WASN'T the first person to rally communities to plant trees in Kenya or the only individual to see reforestation as key to the survival of those communities or protection of natural resources. Trees didn't define her activism, but they were the roots, as it were, that held together her ecosystemic view of the body politic. Trees also helped her construct and project a series of identities that were useful to her and her work, some of which I've already highlighted: Earth Mother; the agronomist and forester who understood deeply the connection between environmental sustainability and grassroots development; the politician, who saw how trees could provide a way to engage communities and develop civil society to raise consciousness and bring about large-scale social change. Her gently held biocentrism and deep concern for the healing of the planet, encapsulated by the Jewish mandate of *tikkun olam*, was one of the qualities that drew Mia and me toward her work.

As part of our conceptualization for her fourth book, *Replenishing the Earth* (a volume I thought might usefully examine what I fancifully called "a spirituality of environmental activism"), Prof and I agreed to explore the sacred meaning of the tree in ancient cultures, and it was my task to conduct the preliminary research. As it turned out, the trails I followed took me deep into the forest and opened up surprising paths.

✳   ✳   ✳

In his fascinating and encompassing work *Forests: The Shadow of Civilization*, Robert Pogue Harrison writes about Gilgamesh, the part-mythic king of the Sumerian city of Uruk in Mesopotomia, who lived around 2700 BCE, and is the subject of one of the world's oldest written epics. Harrison writes that Gilgamesh is called the "builder of the walls of Uruk." Yet, as he looks over the battlements of the city and sees the bodies of the dead citizens floating down the river (a traditional Sumerian funeral ritual), the king worries that he hasn't left a large enough mark on history. He asks Utu, the sun god, to give him permission to slay Huwawa, the forest demon of the Cedar Mountain, so that he can thereby gain glory.

Harrison notes that by this time in the history of Sumer, most of the immediate lumber around Uruk had been harvested, leaving only the forested mountain areas uncut. The killing of the demon is, therefore, an allegory for the dangerous trip that Gilgamesh must make to the mountain to access the timber resources. If he can avoid bandits and wild animals and send the logs down the river to Uruk, he'll thereby gain glory for himself.

Utu reluctantly agrees to Gilgamesh's request and Huwawa meets his end. But the death of the forest demon angers the other gods, since the Cedar Mountain is sacred and the murder of Huwawa thereby sacrilegious. According to Harrison:

> In some versions of the story, Gilgamesh's beloved friend, Enkidu, must pay for the crime of killing Huwawa with his own life. Upon the death of his friend Gilgamesh falls into an exacerbated state of melancholy, consuming himself with thoughts about death. Fame and the monuments of memory no longer console him for the fact of dying. That is why Gilgamesh sets out on another journey, this time in search of everlasting life.

The oldest renderings of the epic of Gilgamesh date from around 2000 BCE, and thus constitute some of the most ancient recorded reflections on what we generally think of as "civilization." Some scholars have credited the Sumerians with the invention of year-round agriculture as well as the development of writing, and from the epic that relates his story and accompanying archeological discoveries it has been determined that the city of Uruk around the time of Gilgamesh's rule contained 80,000 inhabitants. Nevertheless, while he rules at what appears to be the apex of his and his city's power and success, Gilgamesh remains dissatisfied. Harrison adds:

> [T]he long and desperate quest for personal immortality only leads [Gilgamesh] to the knowledge that death is an ineluctable and non-negotiable condition of life—that the cadaverous logs he sent down to the city from the Cedar Mountain cannot spare him his last journey of all down the very same river. And this, at the dawn of civilization, is called "wisdom."

Gilgamesh believes that the forest, the home of the demon, stands in the way of his happiness—not least because it exists outside his control. In other words, for civilization to reach its apogee, Nature, which is the realm of the nonhuman and is therefore uncivilized, must be conquered and controlled. But as Gilgamesh discovers, the destruction neither brings happiness nor security, since once Nature has been de-natured, nothing exists against which civilization can juxtapose itself; the urge to remove ourselves from the natural world to build our cities is balanced by the alienation from and longing for it we feel, once we've achieved mastery over it. Gilgamesh loses his sense of purpose because when he looks from the battlements all he sees is himself: a corpse that was once alive floating down the river. In the end, he realizes, he'll be as dead as the logs he cut in order to render himself immortal.

This story obviously possesses ecological implications as well as psychological connotations. For the city to be constructed and for its inhabitants to be watered and fed, trees must be felled, land cleared for agriculture, and water channeled, pooled, and dammed. When Gilgamesh recognizes that the trunks that pass down the river don't signify life but portend death, he discerns that the project of civilization—the human endeavor to extend itself beyond subsistence alone—inherently contains within it the essence of its own destruction, a logic that in the twenty-first century is becoming ever more evident to us.

Forests: The Shadow of Civilization presents a fascinating overview of the many ways the Western imagination and its various polities have responded to forests—an arc that extends from the worship of sacred groves in ancient Greek and Roman times to preserves for the royal prerogative of hunting in the Middle Ages and early Renaissance; from seclusions where the outlawed and out of favor gather to fight the powers that be to the Enlightenment's reconceptualization of the forest as an extension of the state's control over resources and riches. Harrison observes how throughout European history forests have been both alluring and threatening, a domain of demons and fairies, shape-shifters and the unforeseen. They've been locations where one's original purpose is confused or clarified. Unless one is careful (or perhaps lucky), one can lose one's way should one step off the narrow path marked out by previous travelers and be transformed into something you're not—or, more subversively, become a version of yourself truer than the superficial sophisticate who resides in the city.

More immediately resonant for *The Elephants in the Room*, however, is one European's experience of a forest that occurred at about the same time that Dame Daphne's Great-Uncle Will arrived in British East Africa. It's one of the more influential visions of Africa in the West, in that what it says (and what it does not) display a world-view that both reflects and amplifies the Euro-American vision of the continent. It's a tale that draws attention to a number of metaphorical elephants in the room that loom large over all its protagonists, both fictional and non-. As we'll see in the next couple of chapters, this account has inevitably colored my encounter with the life and work of Wangari Maathai and Daphne Sheldrick.

* * *

In 1902—a few months before Louis Leakey and Prof's father were born and the year the Uganda railway was completed, and millennia after the telling of the tale of Gilgamesh's struggle against Huwawa—the author Joseph Conrad published a story of how another civilization at its apogee undertook another voyage up another river in another forest to bring under control another qua-si-mythic figure. Like Huwawa in the ancient epic, the forest as described by Conrad's main narrator Charlie Marlow in *Heart of Darkness* has a chthonic energy—as old as the "earliest beginnings of the world ... [with] the stillness of an implacable force brooding over an inscrutable intention" (48). The forest always threatens to overwhelm the pitiful outposts of progress (to use the title of another Conrad novella) it surrounds, and the attempt to extract its resources meets with a resistance from the forest that, like Huwawa's, has all the weight and intractability of a curse.

Marlow tells a motley group of men (identified only by their middle-class professions) gathered on the *Nellie*, a cruising yawl anchored in the Thames estuary near London, how through the auspices of his aunt he landed a job commanding a steamboat for an unnamed company that gathered ivory from inland. He relates how shortly after he arrived at the mouth of a great river in the continent, Marlow learned about a Mr. Kurtz, a valued collector of elephant tusks, who was reputed to be an individual of remarkable talent and stirring ideals.

As Marlow in his story makes his way up the river toward Kurtz's station, the mist and cloud that hang above and around the banks befog the truth about the great man and render progress difficult. Eventually, we learn that Kurtz's haul has exacted a terrible price, as his greed for ivory and power has overwhelmed whatever high-minded principles may originally have motivated his civilizing mission. He's acquired at least one African concubine and is being worshipped as a demi-god by a tribe whom he's engaged to attack and scalp another group of natives. Among other unmentioned atrocities, he has placed their shrunken heads on poles around his enclosure. Despite facing resistance from the man himself, his concubine, and his followers, Marlow brings the self-pitying and feverish Kurtz on board and turns his steamer downstream.

Ivory has consumed Kurtz and become the obscene talisman for the moral decay that has corroded every aspect of the venture: "The word 'ivory' rang in the air," says Marlow, "was whispered, was sighed. You would think they were praying to it. A taint of imbecile rapacity blew through it all, like a whiff from some corpse" (33). Kurtz has been whittled into the substance itself: "I could see the cage of his ribs all astir, the bones of his arm waving. It was as though an animated image of death carved out of old ivory had been shaking its hand" (85). Kurtz's hairless head is like "an ivory ball" (69) and his "ivory face [has] the expression of sombre pride" (99).

Marlow ties Kurtz's interior hollowing-out directly to the vast amount of ivory he's accumulated (69). Yet, even within his sickness, Kurtz clings on to the tusks (106), declaring them his own and not the Company's. He's under no illusions as to the real purpose of Marlow's retrieval (88); the Company values his stash more than they do him, although (he claims) he taught them the true worth of what they hunger after. Kurtz craves ownership of the material that he believes gives him enormous power but knows is eating him up from the inside. En route downriver, he demands to be welcomed by the great and the good when he returns to Europe; he was "on the threshold of great things" he states (94). Eventually, he dies, uttering his famous last words, "The horror! The horror!" (100)

Marlow finds out that Kurtz, at the request of the fictional and absurdly named International Society for the
Suppression of Savage Customs, has written a seven-
teen-page report, "vibrating with eloquence," in which
Kurtz avers that for the white man to do good in Africa
he must exert supremacy akin to a supernatural being.
Marlow drily observes that the "moving appeal to every
altruistic sentiment" is short of practical applications,
except for the handwritten statement appended to the
bottom: "Exterminate all the brutes!" (71) Marlow tears
off the addendum when he leaves the report at the company's headquarters. He then visits Kurtz's inamorata, "the
Intended," in Europe and presents her with her fiancé's
box of papers, which Kurtz has entrusted to him. When
she asks Marlow to repeat Kurtz's last words to her, Marlow decides not to tell her the truth and instead professes
that Kurtz spoke her name. These lies perpetuate not only
the self-congratulatory belief in Kurtz held by Marlow's
giddy aunt, the Intended, and all of Europe (which "con-
tributed to the making of Kurtz" [71]), but they allow the
atrocities to continue by maintaining the fiction (and the
company's propaganda) that what is taking place in Africa
is a noble cause and not simply "grubbing for ivory" (61),
as Marlow calls it.

Marlow, whose own health has been compromised by
his journey, is disgusted by the deceptions he practiced on
others and himself and appalled by the greed and hypocrisy of the white men involved in the enterprise. Far from
the virile specimens demanded by *Kenya: Britain's Most*

Attractive Colony, Marlow finds empty shells (one person suggests that "Men who come out here should have no entrails" [31]), ludicrous pencil-pushers, clownish chancers, or devilish desperadoes (prospectors calling themselves the Eldorado Exploring Expedition are likened to "sordid buccaneers" [43]). Marlow retains a grudging respect for those white men who maintain a certain constructed order amid the amoral indifference of the jungle. The sole way to make sense of the task, he says, is through "the idea only ... something you can set up, and bow down before, and offer a sacrifice to ..." (10) or "a desperate belief" (52).

Kurtz, for all his reputation as "a prodigy ... an emissary of pity, and science, and progress" (36), is the emptiest of the lot—an "initiated wraith from the back of Nowhere" (71), a "shadow" (92), "a vapour exhaled by the earth" (93), "a voice," and a "hollow sham" (98). Even so, Marlow agrees with those who've met Kurtz that he is, indeed, remarkable: not because of his promise, generous mind, or noble heart (109), but because he wrestled with his greed and grandiosity, "kicked himself loose of the earth" (95), stepped over the edge, and fell to "the bottom of a precipice where the sun never shines" (99). In his embrace of his own "impenetrable darkness" (99), Kurtz, like Milton's Lucifer ("the bearer of light"), achieves in his descent into the depths a perverse, despairing, and yet fearsome kind of self-knowledge, even in his delusion and degradation.

The genius of *Heart of Darkness* is that, just as Marlow's stuttering, anguished, self-lacerating, and sardonic prose struggles to come to grips with just what it was that Kurtz saw and did, the reader never truly ascertains whether Kurtz was an honorable man who when faced with the elemental forest had no resources to defend himself against its shadowy magnetism, or whether, when confronted by the forest daemon's "otherness," this epitome of *homo civilis* reverted to a primeval self that is always present within us, as Marlow contends, through "the awakening of forgotten and brutal instincts, by the memory of gratified and monstrous passions" (94–5). However one might choose to characterize the balance between the interior or exterior darknesses that permeate the novella, Marlow is contemptuous of the notion that what he disdainfully calls "high and just proceedings" (23) and this "cause of progress" (14) can be achieved within an "immensity" (38) "so impenetrable to human thought, so pitiless to human weakness" (80).

*   *   *

When I was about sixteen, my English Literature and Language class at the boys' boarding school I attended in the U.K. studied *Heart of Darkness*. We explored Conrad's use of unreliable narrators (Marlow and an unnamed voice who bookends the tale) and the several ironies such a strategy evokes. We analyzed the verbal abstractions, hesitations, and evasions by which Conrad keeps full comprehension of exactly what Kurtz had done just beyond reach. We investigated the symbolism of light and dark that provides the novella with its chiaroscuro and evocative, brooding density. We noted that many characters and places seemed indistinct or amorphous, as though the entire journey were shrouded in a dream or mist. We observed how Marlow is at once appalled by and drawn to the depths that Kurtz enters into—"the fascination of the abomination" (9)—and asked ourselves whether the lack of a definite article in the book's title implied not merely a non-specific journey but an uncanny, nightmarish descent into the underworld of the unconscious (Freud's *The Interpretation of Dreams* was published in 1899, the same year that *Heart of Darkness* was serialized in *Blackwood's Magazine*).

I'll admit that my memory of those years is as hazy as Marlow's view of the river. But to the best of my recollection, I don't recall our class actually discussing in any depth the novella's *historical* background—something, reading the book thirty years on, I find astonishing. It's not such a secret. Although Marlow doesn't tell his listeners where in Africa or Europe his story is set, Conrad doesn't disguise the topography, the contemporary relevance of the story, or, in his brief introduction, how much of the story is based on his own personal experience.

Conrad didn't need specifics: they would have been common knowledge to his readers. The river up which Marlow guides his steamboat is clearly the Congo; the territory that Kurtz so ruthlessly exploits is the Congo Free State; and the private company that employs Marlow (and Kurtz) is based in Brussels and owned by Leopold II, King of the Belgians (1835–1909). By the time *Heart of Darkness* was published, the Congo Free State and Leopold II's company had become notorious for the atrocities committed toward, and exploitation of, the peoples of the region. Our English class may, perhaps, have been informed that Conrad had based the book on his six months of navigating a steamer up and down the Congo in 1890, but I don't recall our going into detail about how Leopold's company employed Conrad, and whether what Kurtz did could have had a basis in fact.

The writer Adam Hochschild acknowledges that when he studied *Heart of Darkness* in high school, he too was clueless about the historical origins of Conrad's novella. It was only when he read a footnote in a book as an adult that he learned about the region's past. His magnificent *King Leopold's Ghost*, an examination of how one man fooled the world into allowing him to own a vast area of the African continent and the story of some of the people who exposed him, seeks to fill in that lacuna.

Hochschild writes that Leopold II was keen to insert himself personally into what became known, pejoratively, as the Scramble for Africa. In the second half of the nineteenth century, Germany, Great Britain, France, and Italy carved up the landmass between them: partly to access its natural resources; partly to gain strategic advantage over their fellow European powers; and partly out of a genuine belief in the superiority of their race and civilization and the conviction that it was their self-abnegating obligation to end slavery and encourage development in, and bring Christianity to, the "Dark Continent." This commitment became known, after an 1899 poem by Rudyard Kipling, as the White Man's Burden, and you can hear echoes of it in *Kenya: Britain's Most Attractive Colony*. If you believe economists such as William Easterly and Dambisa Moyo, this self-defined responsibility has bedeviled the conditionalities of aid and its delivery from the industrialized world (known in the language of international development as the global North) to developing nations (the global South). In fact, these economists argue, the assumption of that cause has encouraged unrealistic and, in fact, counterproductive expectations in the former and dependency and political, economic, and social distortion in the latter.

According to Hochschild, Leopold wanted to join the Scramble for his own personal aggrandizement and enrichment, which because of Belgium's financial and constitutional constraints he couldn't undertake *pour la gloire et la patrie*. By the late 1870s virtually all of the land in Africa had been mapped and acquired by the other European powers. Leopold eyed for himself the one remaining area—the vast swath of the Congo Basin, which due to the dense forests that covered the land and the cataracts that made traveling upriver by boat impossible, was unclaimed and uncharted by Europeans. Leopold advanced his cause internationally by insisting he was only seeking control over the territory to allow further scientific exploration, end the slave trade of his contemporary Tippu Tip, and bring the benefits of civilization (medicine, schools, infrastructure) to the region. Financial gain, he insisted, was furthest from his mind.

Leopold duped or hired scientists, explorers, and philanthropists to advocate for him in the well-appointed corridors and staterooms of the European powers. He set up a dummy organization to distract attention from his true aims, and waited patiently for the right moment to act. He employed the famed Welsh-American explorer and journalist Henry Morton Stanley to scout out the Congo Basin, and then charmed and/or paid off various delegations at the Berlin Conference in 1884–5—which the European powers had organized to settle boundaries and determine control in Africa—to concede to him the enormous territory that encompasses roughly what we know today as the Democratic Republic of Congo.

As Hochschild describes in chilling detail, over the next two decades, far from being the enlightened center of non-profit education and uplift for the people, the area called the Congo Free State became a heavily policed, militarized zone almost entirely dedicated to the extraction of ivory and rubber. Leopold's various station agents and their armed forces terrorized the local people. They forced them to work at gunpoint or kidnapped women and children until the communities agreed to provide more ivory or to tap more rubber. The authorities or their accomplices severed hands, cut off noses and ears, and beheaded those who failed to meet the quotas or threatened to rebel. In the Congo alone, untold millions of native Africans died from disease, displacement, and massacres. In 1908, opposition to Leopold's concession had become so fierce, and the news emerging from journalists, human rights campaigners, and other whistleblowers so noxious, that the Belgian government was forced to take it over.

Hochschild makes the point that for all of Conrad's scathing critique of Belgian policies in the Congo Free State, the novelist was hardly a liberal democrat, being a strong supporter of the British Empire. The narrator who frames Marlow's narrative comments approvingly on Britain's tradition of soldier-sailors: "from Sir Francis Drake to Sir John Franklin . . . the great knights-errant of the seas . . . the adventurers and settlers" (7). Marlow takes comfort in a map in the company's offices that color-codes the colonies under British protection. There is, he notes, "a vast amount of red—good to see at any time, because one knows that some real work is done in there" (14).

Conrad's many and subtle uses of irony mean we should be careful about assuming that either Marlow's or the external narrator's point of view is the same as the author's; likewise, we should be cautious about absolving Conrad from politically incorrect positions simply because he shades and shadows his ideas through the scrims of narrators whose version of events may be self-serving and/ or willfully ignorant. But *Heart of Darkness*'s voices do not all speak as one. Marlow, for instance, is a good deal more jaundiced about the glamour or honor of global exploration than the narrator who begins and ends the book: "The conquest of the earth, which mostly means the taking it away from those who have a different complexion or slightly flatter noses than ourselves, is not a pretty thing when you look into it too much" (10).

Hochschild writes that during Conrad's brief time in the Congo captaining his steamer up and down the river, the future author may have encountered several models for agents such as Mr. Kurtz: dissolute and often sadistic opportunists and hypocritical martinets whom the company gave almost entirely free rein to in the forest, and who exploited the absence of any restraining central authority to become more "savage" than the so-called savages themselves. This raises the prospect, not offered directly by Hochschild or my high-school class, that an additional way to read *Heart of Darkness* is not that Kurtz is an exemplum of a refined civilization overwhelmed by the savagery of the natural world and native peoples, or even that he surrenders to the primitive in all of us, but is instead the epitome of the hideous, vengeful moral vacuity within "civilization" *itself.*

Evidence for this reading exists in one of Marlow's most famous metaphors: where he calls the city from which he receives his steamboat commission "sepulchral" (35) and a "whited sepulchre" (14), a phrase originally attributed to Jesus of Nazareth in the King James Bible (Matthew 23:27). Conrad's apothegm looks forward to the bone-yards of the African continent, where everything and everyone appears to have been reduced to their skeletal remains. The six chain-ganged prisoners whom Marlow encounters when he arrives at the head of the river are emaciated: "I could see every rib, the joints of their limbs were like knots in a rope"; a boiler lies "wallowing in the grass . . . as dead as the carcass of some animal" (22). Marlow's predecessor, Fresleven, who'd gone insane and been killed when a native slid a spear between the Swede's shoulder blades, remains unburied, "grass growing through his ribs . . . tall enough to hide his bones" (13). Another group of sickened natives are nothing more than "black bones reclined at full length" (24) against a tree.

Evoking religious relics contained in a tomb whose identity has been either disguised or made presentable, the figure of the whited sepulchre also illustrates the pseudo-piety of Leopold's endeavors and "the philanthropic pretence of the whole concern" (35). It suggests that the construction of civilization itself is an act of plastering over wickedness (Marlow calls one of the agents a "papier-maché Mephistopheles" [37]). Indeed, in his first words to the assembly on the *Nellie* Marlow comments that the great river (and in effect London and England itself) was once "one of the dark places of the earth" (7). These images imply that what we call "civilization" is the mere whitewashing over our inevitable moral and physical decay—a situation that Gilgamesh all those years earlier would recognize. As Marlow notes, it's "the idea only" that sustains the fiction that the exquisite refinements of our gilded age will forever disguise the cankerous putrefaction of bloated bodies, dead wood, severed hands piled high, or tuskless elephants lying dead in the savannah or floating down the river.

*   *   *

Accompanying our class's silence on the historical foundations of Conrad's masterpiece was (as far as I can recall)
a similar non-discussion of the complex issue of race in
Heart of Darkness. Perhaps we were lulled by Marlow's
perplexed respect for the blunt cannibal he meets—an
encounter that leads Marlow to wonder sardonically
whether, unlike some of the other sad specimens of white
men in the tropics, he's healthy enough to be considered
"appetizing" (59). Marlow is sarcastically amused by the
scarified "savage," with a bone "as big as a watch, struck
flatways through his lower lip," who's learned to keep a
steamship going by being told that "should the water in
that transparent thing disappear, the evil spirit inside the
boiler would get angry through the greatness of his thirst,
and take a terrible vengeance" (53).

Elsewhere in the novella, Marlow adopts some of the
humid tropes of French painter Henri Rousseau's roman-
tic primitivism (see, for instance, *The Dream*, 1910). Kurtz's
African concubine, for instance, is "savage and superb,
wild-eyed and magnificent" (87). Marlow's description
of the peoples he sees along the coast foreshadows the
idealized effigies in Leni Riefenstahl's photographs of the
peoples of East and Central Africa and Picasso's reconfiguration of the face of Western art after he saw an African
mask in 1907: "They shouted, sang; their bodies streamed
with perspiration; they had faces like grotesque masks—
these chaps; but they had bone, muscle, a wild vitality, an
intense energy of movement, that was as natural and true
as the surf along their coast" (20).

Marlow, ever the paradox, is less inclined to ridicule the Africans for their barbarisms, if for no other reason than, unlike the white men on the vast continent, "[t]hey wanted no excuse for being there" (20). Indeed, their "naturalness"—"prehistoric" (51), like the forest—is part of the atavistic, elemental attraction that, Marlow suggests, threatens to overwhelm all the constructions of the ordered soul. Marlow comments that the drumming that throbs from the interior elicits "just the faintest trace of a response to the terrible frankness of that noise, a dim suspicion of there being a meaning in it which you—you so remote from the night of first ages—could comprehend" (52).

In spite of these subtle "appreciations" of the Africans, however, few speak in the novella and are often seen acting collectively rather than as individuals. Marlow expresses sympathy for the illnesses and cruelties that are visited upon the Africans, but he also finds them absurd when they attempt to mimic the civilization that's been imposed on them. Marlow shows no curiosity about their customs, except to wonder at their strangeness and their superstitions, and to assume that it exists in opposition to the rational, formally Christian culture from which he comes: "A black figure stood up, strode on long black legs, waving long black arms, across the glow. It had horns—antelope horns, I think—on its head. Some sorcerer, some witch-man, no doubt: it looked fiendlike enough" (94). In fact, to Marlow what the Africans *do* and why they do it seem as impenetrable and mystifying as the forest through which his boat travels.

It seems incredible to me now that Marlow's recurrent use of "nigger/s" would have passed us by. Perhaps our teacher felt that our class of white, upper-middle-class boys would be offended if we discussed the word, although I don't remember anyone voicing unease about our examination of Conrad's short story "The Nigger of the *Narcissus*." It was not as if I, or my classmates, were unfamiliar with black people—although how we *were* familiar with them is depressingly instructive. A few students of Afro-Caribbean descent went to both my prep school, where I was educated from eight to thirteen years of age, and my high school, where I boarded for another five. At my prep school, one long-suffering boy allowed us to touch his hair to see what it felt like; during the years when *Starsky & Hutch* became our favorite show on British television, he was (naturally) renamed Huggy Bear, after the detectives' jive-talking street informant, and subsequently attained a certain cool swagger in our eyes. Another youth was cast as the Prince of Morocco in our high school's production of Shakespeare's *Merchant of Venice*. We were nothing if not consistent in our literalism and essentialism: one of the few Jewish boys at the school played Shylock.

Hard as it is for me to fathom now, we used racial epithets freely and unselfconsciously, including those whose provenance we had little idea of but that wouldn't have taken much effort to locate. When one of us was "gypped," we'd been cheated, because that's what gypsies or "Egyptians" did. We called someone a "nignog" if they'd been stupid, and when a boy had "wogged" something, he'd stolen it: a direct reference to the golliwog caricature of thick lips and bulging eyes. The word was thus (it seems) a byword for untrustworthiness, even though a golliwog took his place among the teddy bears on my bed when I was an infant.

Several of our British television shows and comedians in the 1970s reinforced the idea that the people to whom we'd shown the benefits of becoming like us by occupying their countries shouldn't be in ours; or they could stay if we were allowed to laugh at their accented misuse of English and affirm their "otherness." I enjoyed these shows and found them funny. *The Black and White Minstrel Show*, which consisted of a series of comedy acts and song-and-dance routines with white men in blackface dancing with white women, remained on British television until 1978. I watched it with little sense that this was humiliating or strange.

Even more baffling to me in terms of my own lack of awareness is the fact that, in the same year that my English class studied *Heart of Darkness*, I read *Burmese Days*, George Orwell's scathing attack on the bored, febrile, and hypocritical lives of colonialists and the colonized in the waning years of the British Raj. Published in the year Dame Daphne was born and *Kenya: Britain's Most Attractive Colony* was printed, *Burmese Days* is a story of emotional and moral breakdown in a psychophysical climate in its own way as corrosive as that of Conrad's Congo. Orwell, a socialist, loathed Britain's imperial posturing, and his portraits of the expat mediocrities, racists, and absurd *pukka* and *mem sahibs* drip with contempt. I recall closing the book and sensing that Orwell wanted me to take something harder and more political away from my reading experience than the memory of a doomed and shabby love affair bedewed with the perspiring exoticism of the orient. Yet I wasn't entirely sure what the goings on in northern Burma in the early 1930s had to do with my life. Its concerns felt too remote for a fifteen-year-old at a boys' boarding school (as Orwell had once been), as though it belonged to a time and an era that had passed . . . or perhaps relayed a desperate dissatisfaction with life and desire and their thwarted ambitions into which I'd not yet grown.

❀   ❀   ❀

On reflection, I probably shouldn't be surprised that I was apparently uncomprehending of these stories' political and social realities, as opposed to their psychological or symbolic import; or that I merely valued them as entertainments and not instructive in some way about my economic, social, and racial privilege. The books I devoured as a younger boy included the Belgian Hergé's *Tintin in the Congo* (with its caricatures of Africans as thick-lipped, child-like buffoons) and Frenchman Jean de Brunhoff's stories about Babar the elephant (the bipedal, clothed king of the beasts, who orders his fellow creatures to clear the forest in order to build the tidy little houses of Celesteville). I recollect no questioning of whether such a view of Africa and Africans—bestialized, infantilized, or anthropomorphized—might have changed in the forty years since these books first came out and I read them. Nobody suggested to me that these texts might be inappropriate or out of date.

At eight or nine years old, I became a devoted reader of the series of books by Canadian naturalist Willard Price (1887–1983), which featured a thirteen-year-old American, Roger Hunt, and his nineteen-year-old brother Hal traveling around the world (occasionally with their father, John) catching animals for zoos, circuses, carnivals, menageries, and film companies, and fighting off poachers, corrupt officials, and other ne'er-do-wells who are intent on killing animals and not just capturing them.

Several of these tales are set in East Africa, and I decided to re-read three of them (*African Adventure* [1963], *Elephant Adventure* [1964], and *Safari Adventure* [1966]) before writing this book, on a hunch that they might contain hints about the imaginative world I inhabited forty years ago. Sure enough, in addition to extremely dubious messages regarding our relationship with wildlife and male with female (which we'll explore in later chapters), the three books throw up a miasma as (in)toxic(ating) to one's perspective and awareness of the self and the other as that through which Marlow travels toward Kurtz.

African Adventure draws upon a motif that Kurtz would have recognized: the barbaric and bizarre ethno-religious practices of native peoples who need to be put in their place by, and subjected to the rule of, white people. Complicating the efforts of John Hunt and the boys to capture an array of big game is that Joro, one of their thirty-strong team of African support staff, is a member of the secretive Leopard Society (the name of an actual Mau Mau–like movement that operated in West Africa in the early twentieth century). Joro has been ordered by his fellow Leopard members to kill John and his two sons, or risk the death of his own wife and children. The boys are mystified as to why Joro would want to harm them. It seems senseless. Fortunately, their father is on hand to provide a reason— one that echoes some of the thinking we're familiar with:

It makes African sense. It makes Leopard Society sense. This isn't London. A couple of dozen African countries have become independent during the last few years, and they have parliaments and presidents and delegates to the United Nations, and they are making a lot of progress and we hope the best for them. But that must not blind us to the fact that outside the cities, away back in these forests, life can be as savage as it was a hundred years ago. Ninety per cent of black Africans have never been inside a school. Some of them blame everything on the white man. You've heard of the Mau Mau—the secret society that makes its members promise to kill whites. It was at its worst in 1952 but popped up again in 1958, and now it has become more secret than ever and is likely to go on as long as there are white men in East Africa holding land that the blacks think should belong to them. More than twenty thousand people have been killed by this society. Most of the killers don't want to kill—the society makes them.

This explanation, although short on detail about why the Leopard Society/Mau Mau might harbor resentment toward white people or whether land reform might be a suitable corrective to the situation, seems to satisfy the boys. Joro is as conflicted about the terrible task before him as Kinanda, the singing servant in the Sheldrick household: "The savage was strong and fierce within him," writes Price, "yet also inside him was a very gentle heart that prompted him to protect two leopard cubs and a dog." Joro makes a few PG-13 attempts to kill the boys. In the end, the Hunts blow open the secret society, its members are arrested, and Joro is mightily relieved.

As a comic foil to offset the Hunts' genial condescension, Price creates the character of Colonel Bigg, a loudmouthed Yankee buffoon and blusterer, who in addition to being an overt racist and a bigot, is also (most tellingly for the Hunts, perhaps) incompetent with a firearm, ignorant of animal behavior, and a liar about his hunting skills. Hal and Roger treat him with benign good humor and a preternatural calmness that one would not necessarily count among teenagers' foremost attributes.

Though little given to introspection, the boys try to do the same with the Africans with whom they come into contact. When the chief of a nearby village falls sick with what turns out to be malaria, the local medicine man sug-

gests that he should eat a leopard heart as a cure. Hal is baffled. "But how can you believe this nonsense?" he asks the
chief. "How could a leopard's heart help you? You are educated. You know the new things, you even speak English.
And yet you give in to this foolish old superstition."

> The chief closed his eyes and said gently, "Not all the old
> things are wrong. Not all the new things are true. You
> also have your superstitions."
>   Hal felt like a small boy being gently reproved by his
> father. "Indeed we do have our superstitions," he said.
> "We have much to learn, and we can learn a great deal
> from the people of Africa. Still—I might have something
> in this black box that would help you."

The "something" happens to be quinine.

Although the boys, as Hal admits, may have much to
learn, Price himself seems very sure about the nature of
Africans. "It is easy to scare an African," he declaims in
African Adventure, "but after the danger is over he just as
easily laughs." "The African has his own sense of humour,"
he mentions later on in the same book. "It is tickled by
stories of accidents. He thinks it very funny if someone
takes a tumble—even if the one who tumbles is himself." When an elephant gets stuck in a bog in *Elephant
Adventure*, Price offers a concise observation on African
stoicism: "The men stood looking with open mouths, and
tears rolled down some of the black faces. Africans do not
weep easily." Strangely enough, Price doesn't let us in on

whether he thinks Africans crying over the fate of the elephant is justified, or merely sentimental hogwash.

In the second book, set in the Rwenzori Mountains on the border of Uganda and the Democratic Republic of Congo, the villain of the piece is an Arab who's capturing good-looking Tutsi boys and girls and is exporting them to the Middle East for unspecified but nefarious uses by sheikhs—or "desert rats" as Roger calls them. The offensive activity in this volume is the slave trade (what *Kenya: Britain's Most Attractive Colony* evocatively and tellingly names "black ivory") as it was conducted along the coasts of the Indian Ocean. The trafficking of human cargo outraged many European explorers, missionaries, parliamentarians, and monarchs, especially once the Atlantic trade had been brought to an end in the mid-nineteenth century, and, as we've seen in the Kenya handbook, provided both motivation and pretext for the annexation of those areas where the trade was still taking place.

Safari Adventure, which follows immediately on from *Elephant Adventure* and *African Adventure*, removes the boys to Tsavo National Park and the problems warden Mark Crosby is facing trying to stop the widespread poaching of wild animals (akin to the work of Daphne Sheldrick and her second husband, David). The villain in this book embodies yet another ethnicity and its accompanying stereotype. An Indian judge called Sindar Singh, disguised by a thick beard and false bonhomie, is employing black Africans to run a major poaching ring that's shipping animal tusks, horns, hair, feet, skins, etc. out of Mombasa for markets around the world.

Crosby, who's been gulled into believing that the two-faced and obsequious Singh is an animal lover, is as emphatic as Price on how Africans should be treated, if only because nasty things might happen if you're impertinent. When Roger expresses doubts about drinking the blood-and-milk mixture that the Maasai have drawn from their cattle as a friendship offering, Crosby tells him off: "In Africa you show respect for the Africans. If you don't we have unpleasant incidents like the Mau Mau massacres when even our wives have to carry revolvers and no white man's life is safe."

As in *Elephant Adventure*, the Arabs involved in the shipment of the body parts in *Safari Adventure* are straight out of a casting call for villainous Middle-Easterners. A "long-nosed Arab" runs the trap shop, while a "dark-skinned Arab who looked every inch a pirate" stands on a dhow. The Arabs reveal to the boys a shocking reality that is a theme throughout the three books: "In this country, now that the British have gone, we don't worry too much about the law."

Naturally, the dastardly plot is foiled. The boys sabotage Sindar Singh's various animal traps so successfully that the Africans who depend on the poaching trade for money refuse to work for him, since they're not being paid. Hal doesn't take all the credit for stopping Singh: "We're lucky to have a good crew," he confesses to Crosby. "Being Africans themselves, they know more about African animals than we could learn in a lifetime." Crosby, however, is apprehensive. "That may be so," he replies. "But they're not inclined to do much about it. Put their know-how along with your energy and I believe you'll get somewhere."

By the end of *Safari Adventure*, this happy combination remains only theoretical. When Gazi Tanga, the station master on the Nairobi–Mombasa railroad, asks the boys to come and help deal with a group of man-eating lions who've been causing havoc near his station (another real-life problem that affected the construction of the Uganda railroad in the early twentieth century), Hal politely asks Tanga whether he feels that he and Roger might be able to help. Tanga clearly doesn't yet consider his own people's know-how sufficient. "We will do as you say," he replies. How Hal and Roger handle the man-eaters is covered in *Lion Adventure*.

Although, or maybe because, these three titles were produced so soon after the countries in which they're set achieved independence, they veer uncertainly between a wary hope and paternalistic indulgence of African eccentricity and fear that everything is about to fall apart. *Elephant Adventure*, published in 1964, alludes to the civil conflict occurring in the southern part of the Congo, but Price is aware that his young, male, white readers are unlikely to know or care much about the internal struggles of nations caught in the machinations of the Cold War. Or about the Africans themselves, apparently. Except in the instances of Mali and Joro, whose personhood is only defined by their relationship with the white men (for instance, we never meet Joro's family or see him with them), we learn nothing about the other Africans who are part of the team. They're unnamed and they never speak; we're not told about their skills, courage, or how much they're being paid.

In fact, in reading the books again, I constantly had to remind myself where Hal and Roger came from. Teenagers they may still be, but the boys in *Safari Adventure* are called the "masters" rather than employers of their African squad. In their attitude and behavior they seem more like older, colonial Europeans or patriarchs from the American Deep South than sixties kids from New York City. Price seems to hanker for an older and clearer dispensation, where everyone knew their place and role, and the novels as a whole orient themselves nostalgically toward the former colonial power.

It's difficult for me to say how much impact these books had on me as a boy of nine or ten. I recall more clearly the hold that the historical novels of Alexander Kent (a.k.a. Douglas Reeman), Rosemary Sutcliff, and Ronald Welch had on my imagination when I was a little older. I also don't want to over-encumber these slight works. The purpose, as Price surely intended, wasn't to dwell on just how likely it would be that a thirteen-year-old boy, no matter how self-possessed, would command thirty Africans to do what he said, but to keep the reader moving from country to country, species to species, and incident after incident whereby Hal and Roger could come face to face with large animals, learn several useful paragraphs about their habits and behaviors, and then capture or free them. The chapters are short, the action non-stop, and the boys' unflappable resourcefulness and energy unrelenting.

Yet to read these works now is to be shocked at how casually they assume the superiority of the intellect and worldview of a white child over an adult black man— let alone the fauna of the African continent. These novels are of a piece with the *Boy's Own* magazines of the early twentieth century and a welter of films—like *King Solomon's Mines* (1950), *Mogambo* (1952), and *Hatari!* (1966)— that reinforce a vision of the continent south of the Sahara where the white male marches commandingly through the land with all the energetic insouciance of Daphne Sheldrick's Great-Uncle Will, while Africans behave bafflingly, exotically, childishly, threateningly, or passively in response to their "masters'" command.

*   *   *

This was a part of the worldview from Gilgamesh and Conrad to Orwell and Price that I brought (consciously and unconsciously) to my discussion with Wangari Maathai for her books. I did discuss with Prof what I'd read about Gilgamesh via Harrison and Conrad; but it was a feature of her caution and integrity that, interesting though she might find the concepts, she didn't want to claim any knowledge that she hadn't learned directly or experienced herself. She didn't need to have read either Conrad or the

late Nigerian writer Chinua Achebe's scathing critique of
Heart of Darkness to recognize Europeans' blinkered and
one-dimensional view of Africans, and African women in
particular. She didn't need to have read either Achebe's
Things Fall Apart or Leakey's *Southern Kikuyu before 1903*
to know that African peoples had cultures and histories
that were destroyed by colonialism, or to learn about the
psycho-spiritual damage that such loss had caused. Nor
did she have to be au fait with Achebe's *Anthills of the
Savannah* to recognize the damage that African leaders
had brought upon their own peoples following independence—and how torn a Western-educated African might
feel between loyalty to the promise of one's own nation
state and the allure of security, intellectual freedom, and
an open society that seemed forever out of reach in their
homeland. Prof's decision to stick with what she knew
rather than speculate about what she didn't was a further
reminder to me that her background was scientific and
policy-oriented rather than literary and conceptual. Prof
did, however, repurpose our discussion usefully by recol-
lecting her own journey up the Congo—one that would
cast an altogether different light on the above.

In her capacity as the goodwill ambassador for the
Congo rainforest ecosystem, Prof had flown from Braz-
zaville in the Republic of Congo for two hours before
sailing up a tributary of what Marlow calls the "mighty
big river . . . resembling an immense snake uncoiled" (12),
to an opening in the forest. There, local people, including
Aka pygmies and others from Bantu communities greeted

her (the story appears on pages 37–43 of *Replenishing the Earth*). It was a mixed blessing. She wrote:

> As the people clapped and sang in welcome, I joined them to express my appreciation and gratitude, even though I didn't understand their words. What required no translator, however, was the evidence that in spite of the joy on their faces these people were very poor. Their clothes were in tatters, and their drawn faces and thin bodies showed signs of a hard life in the forest (39).

A French timber company representative then demonstrated to Prof the "sustainable" manner in which his company was harvesting lumber. Prof was impressed that the trees were being cut in such a way that they didn't damage the overall ecosystem or other trees as they fell. Yet she found tears coming to her eyes as a two-hundred-year-old sapele was cut down for her benefit. The emotion surprised her. She wasn't sentimental about using wood. She understood that the natural world provided resources that could be utilized; indeed, it had been the Green Belt Movement's initial *raison d'être* for the women to grow saplings to be cut later on, as long as more trees were planted than felled. Yet she could see that the sapele was not ready to come down; it hadn't stopped providing its ecological services to the forest as a carbon sink, shelter for animals, and provider of oxygen. The company representative told her not to worry. "There are millions of other trees out there in the forest," (40) he said.

What was most frustrating and alarming for Prof about the endeavor was that only thirty-five percent of the tree was used for lumber:

> Our group was taken to another site, where Vietnamese workers were feeding the remainder of the tree into a hot kiln where bricks were being made. Those bricks would be used to build houses nearby for the timber company's workers. The local people took the rest of the wood and turned it into charcoal, which was used as fuel both locally and in distant towns and cities. Thick smoke and ash blanketed the area. (41)

Prof was irritated that so little of the value of the tree made it back to the community, and that the poorest people in the region were literally burning through their assets in a process that would make their own survival more difficult and the effort to combat global warming and protect biodiversity that much harder.

Prof reflected that this episode exemplified yet another instance of how foreign entities were continuing to extract resources from Africa, as they had a century previously. Whether in 1907 or 2007, it was still outside forces calling the shots; whether a hundred years ago or today, the distinctions between private enterprise and the actions of the state were murky. Prof observed that it was a step forward that independent African nations, in collaboration with some European governments and international organizations like the World Bank and the African Union, had asked her to be a spokeswoman to find a way to protect the Earth's "second lung," as the forests of the Congo Basin have been called. But in one of her more jaundiced moods, she asked us rhetorically if the heads of the countries surrounding the Basin really had the best interests of the ecosystem and the peoples who lived within it at heart, or whether they weren't in fact merely using her global celebrity to raise money and jostling to access the considerable mineral and other assets that, in spite of the exertions of kleptocrats from King Leopold to Congolese president Joseph Kabila, remained in considerable quantities beneath or within the soil.

By employing the Vietnamese to make bricks, this company (which, she acknowledged, had more social and environmental awareness than many others operating in the region) was nevertheless still not developing the capacity of the Africans to gain the skills that would provide vital revenue to their communities. Most agonizingly of all, the resources that the Africans *did* have the wherewithal and "permission," as it were, to use—turning wood into charcoal—would ultimately contribute to the demise of their existence and exacerbate the global climate change that would speed up the death of the forest. In short, this scenario threatened to be yet another scramble for Africa—one facilitated, as in the past, by corrupt local officials selling off concessions for a quick buck; African governments eager to gain foreign currency reserves and generate revenue for development and not overly scrupulous in their management; foreign companies working under the rubric of the benevolent, sustainable development of a backward region; and, at the bottom of the heap, ordinary people unable to benefit from the huge wealth that surrounded them, driven by desperation to hand over their riches to someone else and destroy their chance of a future.

Prof understood perfectly well how both Marlow and the French employee who brought down the sapele tree could see the forest as an endless, inexhaustible mass. After all, as Marlow relates at the beginning of *Heart of Darkness*, part of his original attraction to the continent (a function of his "passion for maps" and desire to lose himself "in all the glories of exploration" [11]) was that at its center was the supposedly undiscovered Congo—the darkest heart of Darkest Africa. As we saw in Great Uncle-Will's generation's attitudes toward the vast herds of wildlife they encountered in the terrain whose maps "showed little on their empty faces," if one assumes that what one will see is a blank space to be demarcated by fences and contracts of ownership for the purpose of extracting resources or growing and harvesting commodities—rather than a permeable, subtle, and complex ecosystem—one is predisposed neither to value the individual living beings within that ecosystem nor to assume that the system is finely balanced, or full of animate life, or of inherent value to those who exist within it. It's merely another forest and another group of animals.

Prof refashioned my analysis of what the forest meant and the greed with which various groups sought to exploit it not because the ideas I presented were unfamiliar to her, but because she looked at the forest entirely differently. For her, the natural world was not a place of alienation or hidden horrors. It wasn't something to be conquered or controlled or subtracted from without replenishment and growth. Furthermore, in contrast with Conrad's depiction of the forest as impenetrable and inaccessible, Prof knew intimately the various pathways that took her up and down the hills and across the various streams to and from school in the Central Highlands. In fact, Dame Daphne comments in *Love, Life, and Elephants* that one reason why the Mau Mau insurgents proved so difficult to defeat was because they hid numerous signals amid the foliage that the British forces simply didn't notice: "[A] stick tossed on a path at a certain angle; the leaf of a particular plant left on the ground; a twisted stem, a pebble or two—all conveyed a specific message, as did various sounds, which no outsider could decipher as anything other than the call of a bird or animal" (64).

The forest was full of such signs: an echo of the role of woodlands and wild places as refuges for refugees (Robin Hood or Hereward the Wake, for instance), who, as Robert Pogue Harrison notes in *Forests: The Shadow of Civilization*, were masters of subterfuge and cunning—not simply because they were breaking the law but because they felt that justice itself had been sabotaged: "The guile, tricks, and disguises, in short, the various ruses of deception that characterize the outlaw's strategies, all seem to point to the same fundamental or underlying absurdity, namely the travesty of the law by its presumed custodians" (79).

In the contrast between the *vision* of the forest as a vast and incomprehensible unvariegated mass that threatens transformation and terror, and the *experience* of the forest as an intimate, infinitely suggestive, and expressive multiformity—indeed, a grounding continuity amid the endless flow of existence toward expiration—we see stark differences between what each space delimits as civilized and uncivilized. Within that understanding, therefore, the various identities of Prof and the Green Belt Movement and the extra-legality that defined some of their campaigns (which were, in fact, only illegal in that they challenged the state's undermining of the law and/or appealed to a higher, natural law or the greater good) belong to the forest itself.

For Prof, always one to speak practically, the tragedy of Gilgamesh, *Heart and Darkness*, and the felling of the sapele tree was located in our loss of contact with the essential lessons given to us by Huwawa—the representative of all that the forest offered. Huwawa was not the enemy of civilization but its custodian, to be left alone and protected not because he presented a threat but because he was the only bulwark against our tendencies to ruin ourselves. Huwawa was the guardian of potable water, the guarantor of fertile terraces, the provider of clean air, and the first line of defense against the encroaching deserts. Because Prof saw the forest *and* the trees, she could detect a future whereby the ecosystem would no longer sustain itself and what once was thought to be inexhaustible would, literally and metaphorically, go up in smoke.

Indeed, in a reversal of Conrad's vision of the relatively intact Congo Basin as a "gloomy circle of some Inferno" (24), she told us more than once that the charcoal fires and the brick furnaces that consumed the forests she saw in the Congo were her definition of hell.

4

. . . The Seed of Commonwealth, the Germs of Empires

IT WOULD BE easy for me to dismiss my inherent biases and prejudices about Africans and the African continent as simply childish naivety. When it came to the studying of literature, my high school English teacher—who'd been taught in university by professors schooled in textual criticism—eschewed bringing biographical or historical information to the work and instead encouraged readers to examine the text as a self-standing artifact, although neither he nor we were averse to indulging in psychological analysis. (When I went to university a few years later, critical theory and New Historicism were in vogue, and my essays were full of detailed explorations of the political activity and social structures surrounding works of literature.) Perhaps the teacher felt that giving such context to the novella was the job of the history professor, or old news and no longer relevant—even though, when we were reading these works, Zimbabwe was newly independent, Hong Kong was still under the British flag, and Congo's first president, Patrice Lumumba, was only two decades dead.

Such justifications aside, my lack of conscientization argues for a more unsettling conclusion, which is that my fellow classmates and I didn't want to face these legacies and the beliefs that buttressed them. My secondary education valued the kind of tough, unquestioning regimentation that Daphne Sheldrick and Wangari Maathai would have recognized in their own schools, all products of the British imperial system. We were expected to tolerate being away from home and to obey arbitrary rules without question. We found to our cost that bucking the system met with a beating. Prof and her fellow classmates were thrashed if they spoke in their native tongue. A student, as one of my teachers succinctly put it, was best thought of as a sponge: absorbing all the information given to him and then squeezed during examinations. That information involved being silent about those things that weren't to be spoken of and commandingly eloquent about those that were.

In some inchoate way my class (in both senses of the word) believed Marlow when he implied that the British Empire, upon which we were reliably informed the sun had once never set, was different than the other dispensations: fairer, more hard-working, less bloody, more *decent*. Our history lessons failed to inform us that while Leopold II was busy earning a fortune in the Congo, Cecil Rhodes was expanding his mining empire throughout southern Africa. For almost the entire length of my education, the language within which *our* legacy of conquest was couched either neutralized or celebrated British actions—particularly if they were royalist and imperial. In line with the external narrator's enthusiasm for the British seafaring tradition in *Heart of Darkness,* Francis Drake and Walter Raleigh's seizures of gold and silver bullion in the sixteenth century weren't the acts of pirates but of brave privateers. The East India Company was, in its own fashion, every bit as mercenary and beyond the control of democratic or parliamentary control in its dealings with local peoples as Leopold's private business, yet the uprising among Muslims and Hindus in India in 1857, which brought the East India Company to an ignominious end after a quarter of a millennium of existence, was considered a *mutiny* against the British rather than a struggle for self-determination from those who'd been victims of the company's highhandedness and its annexation of wealth, property, and land.

I learned about the horrors of *thagi* (ritualized robbery and assassination) and *sati* (wife-burning) in India in the nineteenth century and "The Black Hole of Calcutta" (another heart of darkness), where in 1756 Britons died of suffocation in a cell at the hands of the insurgents. But I don't recall our studying the British revenge killings or the razing of Delhi that followed the ending of the Indian rebellion a century later, so brilliantly exhumed in William Dalrymple's *The Last Mughal*. We certainly didn't continue to examine British rule in the subcontinent or the 1919 massacre at Amritsar in northern India, where British troops gunned down 379 unarmed demonstrators. We didn't investigate the opium wars of the early 1840s or the follies of the Afghan campaigns. We knew that Florence Nightingale had begun the nursing profession during the Crimean War of the 1850s, but we had little understanding of why Britain was fighting in that part of the world in the first place. Nor did we confront the bitter and enduring legacies of the imperial Great Game as it was played out in the Levant and Mesopotamia before and after World War I.

More pertinently, quite a few of us had very personal reasons for remaining silent. Although I came of age in Britain during the rebellious late 1970s, when the United Kingdom struggled with unemployment, youth disaffection, race riots, and other consequences of its post-imperial decline, for all my later adoption of an insubordinate or subaltern view of Rule Britannia, I had a personal stake in the Empire, as well as the Commonwealth that succeeded it.

My mother's father, after whom I'm named, had two cousins, Peter and Jimmy Moxon. During World War II, Peter joined the army and was posted to Kenya and

Nyasaland (which became Zambia following independence). After retiring from the British army, Peter bought a farm in Malawi, met a Chewa woman named Agatha from Nankumba, married her, and had three children. Jimmy, who never married, moved in the 1940s to what was to become Ghana, where he worked in the colonial civil service before rising to be a district commissioner. He remained in the country after independence in 1957 and was appointed by President Kwame Nkrumah as the minister for information. Jimmy retired in 1963 and ultimately was elected an African chief. He ended up as something of a curiosity and celebrity, even being profiled on the American television show *60 Minutes*.

Jimmy and Peter weren't the only members of my family who became settlers. Leslie Pope, one of my father's uncles on his mother's side, emigrated to Saskatchewan in Canada at the turn of the twentieth century. Like Dame Daphne's relatives, Leslie coped with harsh terrain, a difficult climate, and very few amenities as he attempted to eke out a living on the plains. Like many expats, Leslie considered himself British. He returned to fight in the Great War for the Crown, and like Jimmy and Peter, he stayed on in his adopted country.

In 1941, one of Leslie's English nephews, eighteen-year-old Geoffrey, signed up to fight for his country and was posted, as Peter and Jimmy were, overseas. After stopping off at Durban in South Africa (where he was told in no uncertain terms, and to his amusement, that he mustn't consort with the native women), Geoffrey ended up in

Ferozepore (modern-day Firozpur) in the Punjab, on the border between India and what would become Pakistan. Geoffrey taught physical education to young Sikh, Muslim, and Hindu recruits, and received an early lesson in the complexities of different religions and cultures and how they might, or might not, coexist peaceably.

Geoffrey was allowed to sail to England on compassionate leave following the death of his father in 1945 (his mother died five years later) but returned to India shortly thereafter. He was present at the border during the terrible violence that was unleashed when India and Pakistan were partitioned in 1947. He saw bodies piled by the railroad tracks he was ordered to defend and scavenging birds of prey so gorged on human flesh that they were unable to fly. Geoffrey envisioned no future for himself in civilian life following the war and remained in the army, serving in Germany in 1948 and with the United Nations forces in Korea in 1953–4. He commanded a regiment in Malaysia during the communist uprising in the mid-1960s, and retired in 1978 with the rank of full colonel.

Geoffrey was my father.

Dad was immensely proud to have received the king's (and then queen's) commission, and to have served the Crown for thirty-seven years. He had no problem with the decision to drop bombs on Hiroshima and Nagasaki, since, he argued, it prevented him and tens of thousands of others from a potential bloodbath in any putative invasion of Japan. He thought that, on balance, the Indian subcontinent had been better ruled under the British flag than not. These cursory observations were the extent of my father's effort to explain to me what the Empire meant to him beyond a commitment to keep the railroads running and a genial if distant *noblesse oblige* for the people he commanded.

Like Prof and Daphne Sheldrick (at least as she appears in her book), Dad was neither particularly reflective nor given to re-examining his motives or actions: The world was for doing things in rather than agonizing over. When I worked with Dad on his own memoirs in the 1990s, I pressed him to tell me more of what he'd seen: Berlin at the time of the airlift, Korea in the wake of the devastating conflict on that peninsula, Malaysia in the mid-1960s. Although part of me hoped my father would provide compelling details about what he'd seen, unfurl entertaining anecdotes about the escapades that a hot-blooded young man might have gotten into in foreign parts, whisper about his moments of doubt . . . if I'm honest with myself, another part of me didn't want to know. I wanted him to remain my *gemütlich*, Urdu- and Malay-speaking, gentle father. Although in my teens I rebelled against his identity as a retired army officer by caricaturing him as a contemporary Colonel Blimp (after David Low's wartime cartoon of an old, reactionary soldier), it was hard for me to believe that he would have harmed a fly, let alone killed a man . . . or many. And even though I wished to separate myself from his past, I couldn't help but accommodate myself to his worldview by, for instance, making him laugh as I copied a white comedian's stereotyped West Indian accent. I meant nothing by it; it was all in good fun, wasn't it?

In his letters home, my father comes across as self-assured and slightly arrogant—as comfortable it seems in commanding his twenty or thirty native men as Willard Price's Hal Hunt is with his. When I read Dad's letters, I have to remind myself how young he is when he's writing them, and how unschooled he is about the world into which he's been plunged. Was that bravado a necessary front—both to assure his parents and sister back home in bomb-wracked, depressed, and rationed Birmingham that he was safe, and to ensure that his authority wasn't questioned either by himself or his men lest the delicate façade of the virile colonialist crumble?

How pressing that latter concern might be is clear from that archenemy of empire, George Orwell. Like my father, great-uncle, and grandfather's cousins, Orwell sought work overseas (an experience he drew upon for *Burmese Days*). In his essay "Shooting an Elephant," Orwell describes how as a subdivisional police officer he was ordered by a superior to shoot an elephant in musth—the periodic spike in testosterone that causes bulls to act unpredictably and sometimes aggressively. The elephant had killed a local and was rampaging around the bazaar. Orwell, who confesses he was "young and ill educated," writes of his deep unhappiness at being in Burma. He hated the British Raj's numerous acts of cruelty and its oppression of the native population. Yet he also loathed being the subject of local peoples' ridicule and contempt, which he found deeply upsetting, not least because those (including the religious) who'd laugh at him, trip him up, and insult him were unaware of and indifferent to his own hatred for the regime of which he was an officer. He writes:

> With one part of my mind I thought of the British Raj as an unbreakable tyranny, as something clamped down, in saecula saeculorum, upon the will of prostrate peoples; with another part I thought that the greatest joy in the world would be to drive a bayonet into a Buddhist priest's guts. Feelings like these are the normal by-products of imperialism; ask any Anglo-Indian official, if you can catch him off duty.

Orwell doesn't want to kill the elephant, but he hamfistedly pumps slug after slug into the creature because he sees no other option:

> The people expected it of me and I had got to do it; I could feel their two thousand wills pressing me forward, irresistibly. And it was at this moment, as I stood there with the rifle in my hands, that I first grasped the hollowness, the futility of the white man's dominion in the East. . . . To come all that way, rifle in hand, with two thousand people marching at my heels, and then to trail feebly away, having done nothing—no, that was impossible. The crowd would laugh at me. And my whole life, every white man's life in the East, was one long struggle not to be laughed at.

My father was Hal Hunt's age when he shipped out to India; Leslie was barely any older when he went off to Canada. What did they know? Or indeed, what do any of the young men know as they arrive in warzones or societies amid cultures and languages they do not understand and have no connection with? When you seek the approbation of higher-ups or the approval of your peers and they ask you to quell the uprising, if all you have is a fear of your own humiliation at the hands of those who outnumber you and whose baffling and (in your eyes) undeserved ridicule of you calls into question your own sense of superiority or masculinity or both, it's hardly surprising that you find yourself acting in a manner you might otherwise find alien and abhorrent, or clinging onto archaic notions of your supposed superiority or inherent decency, or hating those who've either made you betray your values or realize that those principles you held so dear are all-too-easily shucked off in the pressure of the moment. Is Kurtz merely the extreme end of a continuum that at some point may include my father, and which Marlow and I in our own stuttering manner have alluded to only to hide it within the abstractions of the unknowable, the unfathomable, the impenetrable—or one's own family's literally unspeakable acts?

*   *   *

I'm fully aware that throughout this book I've poked fun at the slap-on-the-back heartiness of *Kenya: Britain's Most*

Attractive Colony. It's all too easy for me to do the same with *Love, Life, and Elephants'* descriptions of endless vistas, wondrous dawns, love scenes beneath the stars, and the exoticism of the African bush. These give Dame Daphne's story an out-of-time as well as out-of-place tone: a lace-handkerchiefed farewell to a world where well-meaning white people knew what was best for everyone. Even the author's honorific, which signifies that she is Dame Commander of the Order of the British Empire, has an antiquarian cast, a leftover of an imperial entity that no longer exists.

It's true that, as in Willard Price's adventures, few *individual* black Africans (as opposed to various tribes) are named or even present in *Love, Life, and Elephants*. Dame Daphne doesn't go into any detail about how the African keepers manage to stay with the animals in the orphanage when they have families of their own. One attendant, Mischak Nzimbi, has been employed or involved with the Sheldricks for many years, perhaps decades, but we don't hear directly how he feels about the animals he's cared for. And one would wish that *Love, Life, and Elephants* had ventured a little into the turmoil with which Prof was engaged, the efforts to engage more black Africans in the conservation movement, and how the Kenya Wildlife Service might have functioned subsequent to the transition to black-majority rule. (At times, the KWS in the book seems to operate in its own universe.)

For all these observations, however, there's something cheap and petty about a critique that ignores the hard work and genuine investments that Dame Daphne's and other families—including my own, extended one—made in the various countries where they settled. Dame Daphne (it feels too bold an intimacy or petulant a rebuke to remove the honorific) seems to have enjoyed the wonders of the natural world more than crinoline and gins and tonic at the Club. She makes it clear that her stern Scottish ancestry had no truck with the aristocrats and playboys of the Happy Valley set of Kenya's colonials memorialized in the film *White Mischief*.

More seriously, insurgents didn't threaten to destroy all that my family had built up over forty years, as they did with Dame Daphne's aunts and uncles. The Chinese Malay *amah* who looked after me when I was a baby in Kuala Lumpur, Malaysia, hadn't been told to kill me or face her own family's death, as happened with the servant Kinanda. It's impossible to imagine the pain of losing to poaching an animal whom you kept alive and reared for years—and to do it over and over again—and not to feel some kind of blanket resentment and animosity toward those whom you're fighting against and who may be your neighbors.

It would also be dishonest not to recognize that not all military men were like the bigoted Colonel Bigg of *African Adventure*, or explorers like the almost sociopathic Henry Morton Stanley (who did so much of Leopold II's dirty work for him). Nor were all the monastics and evangelists who went to Africa Bible-thumping fundamentalists bent on destroying local cultures. White missionaries, as well as radicals and aristocrats, were active campaigners against the slave trade, as Adam Hochschild so ably illustrates in *Bury the Chains*, his history of the English abolitionist movement. Black and white American and European men and women spoke out against the violent exploitation of local people in Leopold's colonies. They protested the creation of the Uganda railroad as a "white elephant" and championed African independence. *King Leopold's Ghost* reveals that impassioned, selfless resistance to the exploitation of the Congolese came from an ordinary number-cruncher, like the shipping clerk E. D. Morel, and the urbane civil servant and imperial officer Roger Casement, both of whom were instrumental in uncovering and publicizing the evidence that would ultimately damn Leopold II.

Nor was the continent itself a paradise before the arrival of the Europeans. Although, as Wangari Maathai argues in *The Challenge for Africa*, the land south of the Sahara had defined, complex societies that were destroyed after the arrival of the Europeans, Hochschild makes clear in *King Leopold's Ghost* that both white and Arab slavers relied for their business at least initially on African kingdoms' selling of other Africans into bondage. It was a wedge that ultimately would destroy the moral and political foundations of a number of societies throughout the continent. Conflict, sometimes bloody and involving the severing of hands, took place between micro-nations in central Africa independent of the depredations of Leopold's colony. Prof herself notes that her Maasai great-great-grandmother did not join the Kikuyus of her own free will but was abducted. The differentiation between darkness and light, evil and good, is more a matter of illuminating and casting shadows. It would be as inaccurate to assume that, *pace* Marlow, all of Europe was a whited sepulcher as it would be to claim that the entire continent of Africa was a heart of darkness.

Like Leslie Pope and Geoffrey Rowe, Dame Daphne's relatives before her had hankered for greater opportunities and a wider space in which to stake their ground and build their lives. For Jimmy, Peter, Leslie, and my father, the advent of war and the British Empire's global reach not only stirred their patriotism but offered them a chance to travel—an immediate way out, in my father's case, of a life of genteel poverty and diminished prospects, given his lack of academic smarts and money; an escape from an industrial city experiencing the daily deprivations of the Great Depression and post-war austerity.

In Dad's choice to live outside his mother country for years at a time, one can hear the echoes of Great-Uncle Will, Leslie Pope, and a host of other British men—idealistic as well as opportunistic—who wanted to flee the confines of class and tamped-down dreams and forge a future elsewhere, and who took an offer they couldn't refuse. Something of the complexity of these settlers' lives can be glimpsed in Dame Daphne's bitterness in *Love, Life, and Elephants* at how she and other pioneers were treated by the British armed forces and the government in London. You can hear it in the conversation Tony, a warden from the Lake Victoria region, has with Crosby in Willard Price's *Safari Adventure*:

"Nice to see there's a bit of England left in Kenya," said Tony. "I rather expected that by this time I'd see an African behind that desk."

Crosby laughed. "It will happen one of these days. Now that this country has its own government, official jobs like yours and mine will sooner or later be given to Africans."

"Are you going to wait for it to happen? Or resign now?"

"I'll wait. For two reasons. One is that there's no African yet with enough training to take over my job. The other reason is personal. I'd rather take my chances here than face going back to England. What would I do there? I couldn't get a job. They'd ask me, 'What experience have you had?' 'Well, I've been a game warden in Africa.' What use is that in England?"

*   *   *

During the question-and-answer session that followed Dame Daphne's talk at the American Museum of Natural History that night in May 2012, a Maasai man named Ole Kantai from Narok in Kenya addressed Dame Daphne in Kiswahili, the national language of Kenya and Tanzania. He expressed his gratitude that she was speaking on the animals' behalf because, he said, they don't have a voice. But, he wondered, why didn't she come more often to the Masai Mara National Reserve in the southwest of Kenya to help the animals there? Dame Daphne replied in halting Kiswahili that the Trust rescued orphans from the Mara and took them to Nairobi. In English, she then related how these orphans completed their rehabilitation in Tsavo.

As this conversation took place, I wondered to myself whether Dame Daphne's interlocutor wasn't in fact testing her, rather than indicating discomfort with his English. Was Ole Kantai asking her, in effect, to demonstrate how "African" she was: not only in whether she was able to speak Kiswahili but whether she'd be willing in this particular setting (a lecture hall in an Anglophone country) to pay him the respect of responding to him as a *fellow African*? Was he inquiring, *How committed are you to the country you live in? Are you more committed to it than the language you speak?* If I'm correct, then by responding in Kiswahili before returning to English, Dame Daphne was telling him that she was African *enough—enough* that he should appreciate what she'd accomplished on *their* behalf.

Curiously, the audience applauded after Dame Daphne had responded, in spite of the fact that very few of us in the audience would have understood more than a fragment of her answer. Why did we clap? Was it relief that in this exchange our worry about whether this work was *okay* with the "Africans" had been allayed? Had this conversation eased our post-colonial, politically correct sensibilities about the right apportionment of concern among Africans, the animals, and the land that they inhabited? Had this communication demonstrated satisfactorily for us that, forty-five years on from Willard Price's books about the continent, black Africans cared about the animals, too?

Dame Daphne's switch from Kiswahili to English symbolized for me that uncertainty regarding her place—both in time and space—that characterizes *Love, Life, and Elephants*: nostalgia for a time when wildlife was numerous and Kenya was a colony under white rule, and the reality of her situation in a post-colonial state where the animals are under assault from a different group of hunters. Perhaps that's why I feel sympathy for her. She may have expressed her anxieties sometimes in as unfortunate a manner as the nervous wardens Tony and Mark Crosby in *Safari Adventure*, but what would Britain have offered her (or Tony and Mark), if she'd decamped to her ancestral homeland in 1963? A job behind a desk or managing a zoo in a country with no wilderness left? How many "safari parks" could a nation like Britain really sustain, and wouldn't they simply be third-rate facsimiles of what she and her two husbands had worked so hard to develop?

Furthermore, having for over two decades myself lived in New York City—that beacon for refugees from old worlds and unraveler of the straitjackets and winding cloths of history and religious hatred—I can understand how you might want to escape the conformity of familial and class expectations for an open horizon, where you're free to start again with a new identity and destiny. I also know how, paradoxically, you might find it valuable as a psychological bulwark to bring aspects of your prior self with you, allowing yourself to be *in* a place but not quite *from* it. I appreciate how you might want to remain with your clan, with its argot and cultural norms, and become more patriotic toward and nostalgic for your rosily remembered homeland than when you couldn't wait to get out. I can also comprehend how these might be disturbing or alienating to those who are now your neighbors.

What we—Great-Uncle Will, Uncle Leslie, Jimmy and Peter, my father, and I—cannot ignore or play down is that we were able to move elsewhere because, at least in part, three centuries of British men before us had plowed the sea-lanes; a British government had sent gunboats to protect the British ships as they arrived in British ports established by British merchant interests in British colonies, where we were offered land or a job or both in a language all of us could understand. In other words, although we made our homes in many other places, we always had another "home" that was looking after us and to which we could go if the situation became too difficult, or we failed, or we went native or insane. And if we went wrong or let the side down, a Marlow—a man of the "right type"— could always be dispatched to make his way upstream to reclaim us.

In spite of the worries she expresses about being neither British nor Kenyan, Dame Daphne in *Love, Life, and Elephants* emphasizes her loyalty to Queen and Country, even though she's lived her entire life in Kenya. Her knighthood—the first to be bestowed in her homeland since independence in 1963—illustrates that, in spite of the anxieties that she and others may have felt about her life during and after the Mau Mau rebellion, and the betrayals of the British government of their own kind, when push has come to shove, Daphne Sheldrick, my various relatives, and I were (and are) never beyond the reach of the revenging or ennobling sword of the British head of state, under whom we are subjects and whose words in our passports request that we be allowed to move without let or hindrance through the world. In the end, each of us is able to say—including Marlow and the deracinated Franco-Polish Englishman who begat him—with some pride or irony but also with a fair degree of confidence in its consequentiality, *Civis Britannicus Sum*.

5

Tooth and Nail

THE TOPICS OF race and Britain's imperial past weren't the only elephants in the room that our English class's analysis of *Heart of Darkness* avoided. What neither Marlow, Adam Hochschild, nor we schoolboys delved into is the ivory trade itself. In this chapter and beyond, we'll return to the American Museum of Natural History to examine the commitments Dame Daphne made to those other African residents—the animals—and explore the fate of the real elephants whose tusks were the focus of Kurtz's greed as well as the possessions of the animals displayed by Dame Daphne on the video screen in the room that night.

In her lecture, Dame Daphne told us how she'd grown up on a large farm in the Rift Valley within a landscape filled with wildlife and a family of naturalists who loved animals. She'd had contact with the "domestic variety," as she called them—cats, dogs, pigs, sheep, cattle, etc.—but she'd also come to know wild animals, including an orphaned bushbuck, whom she'd been allowed to take care of when she was only three or four years old. Although she was heartbroken when the antelope heard the call of the wild and vanished, Dame Daphne reported that she'd learned an important lesson: "My parents always told me that wild animals never belong. They're only on loan for as long as you need them. And if you love an animal, you must set it free."

Dame Daphne related that her brother had also loved nature and became a warden in Kenya's first national park, Nairobi National Park, which opened in 1946. Through him, she met another warden by the name of Bill Woodley, whom she married in 1953 when she was eighteen. She gave birth to her elder daughter two years later. Bill was transferred to Tsavo, which is between Nairobi and Mombasa, and as he worked to shape the nascent national park there, the couple grew apart. Bill fell in love with someone else, Dame Daphne commented matter-of-factly, and she fell in love with another warden, the naturalist David Sheldrick, whom she met through Bill. "I'm a great believer in destiny," she said. "I had to first marry Bill in order to get to David."

David Sheldrick was to become the love of her life. At Tsavo, David looked after elephant babies who'd been abandoned by their families or orphaned by poachers, which was already a concern in the 1940s. Most of these babies had lost their mothers when they were two years or older, which meant they weren't so in need of the milk that infant elephants have to drink to live. However, some were younger, and they would invariably die in spite of the constant care they were given. In the course of helping her husband over many years, Dame Daphne discovered that coconut milk possessed the necessary caloric content (as opposed to cow's milk or human infant formula, which had been used until then) to enable these very young baby elephants to survive without their mother's milk.

David died prematurely of a heart attack in 1977 at the age of fifty-six, and his wife was devastated. The Kenyan government gave Dame Daphne permission to build a small house in Nairobi National Park. The Nairobi Zoo asked her to look after their orphaned baby elephants, a task that necessitated her driving three hours back and forth each day between the park and the zoo. Her presence was necessary because the babies became used to her, and her alone, providing the care and attention they required.

Poaching for elephant tusks, rhinoceros horn, and numerous animal parts grew worse in East Africa throughout the 1950s, 1960s, and 1970s, and more and more orphaned baby elephants were being delivered to Nairobi Zoo. Dame Daphne informed the zoo's director that she wasn't going to continue driving through the park day and night to care for the orphans, and that she needed to be able to look after them at her house. This is how the Trust's nursery began.

Dame Daphne recruited a team of keepers who could replicate the intense bonding that the babies had lost when they'd been separated from their mothers. She had to employ enough attendants, she told the audience, to be able to rotate them through the herd so that the baby elephants wouldn't become too attached to one person. An elephant's lifespan mimicked humans, she emphasized, to the extent that a ten-year-old elephant calf was as psychologically mature as a ten-year-old human child. Likewise, an infant elephant was as vulnerable and in need of social contact as human babies—perhaps even more so, given that they may have been deeply traumatized after witnessing or experiencing the death of their mother and loss of their larger family. This was why the keepers stayed with the orphans day and night for many months, even years. Without an equally trusted assistant to take the place of a keeper who was on holiday or absent, the elephant could experience psychological distress. This in turn would lead to physiological problems such as diarrhea (which was especially debilitating for an elephant), and the baby would enter a steep decline in health and die.

She'd seen it happen on several occasions, she said, and she'd personally been responsible for the death of an elephant or two because she'd underestimated how sensitive the young ones really were. "The most important thing for an elephant is the family," she asserted. "They have the same sense of family as us, they have all the same emotional traits, and they have many other things that you see in your own children: a little bit of jealousy, competitiveness. They're all individuals in their own right; they all have different personalities. . . . Elephants can teach us humans so much about nurturing and care," she declared. "All the females love the orphans and the babies."

"I often think to myself, there's been such a lot of heartbreak and difficulty throughout the years in raising these elephants; with every one that dies I cry buckets of tears," she reflected. "But actually [I've] seen the elephants and how they live their lives, and all the hardship that they suffer every single day, and the losses that they suffer, and how they grieve and mourn for every single one, and how painful it is for them, but how they have the courage to turn the page and focus on the living. And a lot of people say to me, 'How do you carry on, when there's so much tragedy and you lose so many of them?' And the answer is that I try to do it like the elephants. You grieve and you mourn; that has to be. You bury that one, and you focus on the next one. Because there are going to be others that need your help."

To applause from the audience, Dame Daphne told us that she'd by now raised over 140 elephants and released them into the wild. Ex-orphans who'd gone through the Trust's rehabilitation program (a process that could last as long as ten years) and had been set free in Tsavo National Park often visited the new arrivals at the rehabilitation center, she said. When those arrivals felt confident enough to try a taste of the feral, the ex-orphans would reappear as if from nowhere and usher them from the stockades where the orphans spent the night, and bring them back if the recent graduates didn't feel ready to join their wild brethren forever. These ex-orphans, Dame Daphne added, were often intermediaries between the completely wild animals and the keepers.

Dame Daphne marveled at the extraordinary emotional depth and complexity of elephants. Over the years, many of the female ex-orphans who'd become mothers in the wild had brought their babies back to the compound to share them with the human family who'd raised them at the rehabilitation station. She continued:

> When Yatta had her baby early this year, she came back to the compound with fifty other elephants. Most of them were ex-orphans, all crowding around the little baby: loving it, caring it, touching it with the trunk, all wildly excited. And amongst them were wild friends, too. And these wild friends really have no reason to trust or like humans. But they have to have been told by the ex-orphans, "These guys are OK. These are our friends." Because the elephants encouraged the keepers to actually go right into the herd, and to handle this little newborn calf, which is only a day old, as it sheltered beneath its mother. And that's the greatest accolade you can get from the orphans themselves, a "thank you" for having raised them with tender loving care, and never having brutalized them.

The keepers, she noted, never carried any weapon, "not even a twig." It was a set of relationships based on complete trust. Sometimes the level of communication among the animals was uncanny. On one occasion, she said, the ex-orphans knew before the human attendants when trucks carrying new arrivals were going to show up at the orphanage. Based on her experience over many years, she was sure that elephants possessed psychic ability.

Elephants weren't the only animals on her or her audience's mind that evening. Dame Daphne mentioned that the orphanage had looked after other species, such as antelopes and black rhinoceroses. Rhinos, she said, were easier to rear than elephants but harder to rehabilitate, since they were very territorial. A rhinoceros in the wild knew its physical location and its place in rhino society through smelling the dung and tasting the urine of other rhinos. A gland at the roof of the rhino's mouth enabled the animal to ascertain everything it needed to know about the other rhinos—whether they were bulls or cows, young or old, stranger or friend, even their relative ranking in the herd. The heavily stratified society meant that it took years for a rhinoceros to find its place and not be vulnerable to attacks from other rhinos: such precise knowledge, acquired over a considerable period of time, meant life or death for the animal.

"I think to myself, 'Why do humans think that they're above the animal kingdom?'" Dame Daphne said. "We are, after all, animals, and I think not very successful ones, really. If suddenly all the lights went out in the world, how many of us would be able to survive in a wild situation? We've sort of stepped out of nature. And when you live in a wild place, it's solace. You're at peace with nature; you can learn so much about it. And the best thing of all is that you're never actually on your own; there's always something to interest you, always something to learn from, always something to wonder and marvel at."

Dame Daphne concluded her lecture on a somber note. The work was hard. Poaching and the bushmeat trade—the killing of wild and sometimes endangered animals for food to be sold in markets in urban areas throughout Africa and abroad—were placing enormous strains on animals, and the resources the Trust possessed were limited. There were only so many snares that her rangers and others could pick up or acreage her spotting plane could surveil. In recent years, the Trust had begun to focus on operating anti-poaching teams and establishing mobile veterinary units, and working with the local communities to protect the natural environment and resolve human–wildlife conflict. It was, she admitted, "a sort of holding action, until people are more enlightened about the environment and take more care of it."

*   *   *

As I observed in the first chapter, Dame Daphne states very early on in *Love, Life, and Elephants* how shocking her ancestors' attitudes towards the killing of wildlife, including elephants, may seem to us today. In the book, she's at pains to note that the hunters who preceded her also admired the size and grandeur of individual animals, but, unlike Dame Daphne, they saw them—like the fictional Hunts in Willard Price's books—as creatures whose magnificence meant that they *had* to be taken, not least because serious money was to be made.

Colonel Bigg is in some ways a parody of the Great White Hunter as exemplified by Clark Gable in *Mogambo* and Ernest Hemingway *passim*—the ornery and singular man's man, whose "wise use," "harvesting," and "culling" of species (to employ some of the more common euphemisms for "killing animals") are intended, perversely, to protect these animals from extinction. The Hunter (Willard Price capitalizes the type), who embraces his natural self by relishing the dangers of the bush and judiciously slaughtering fauna, has a long and storied history in the United States and with the American Museum of Natural History in particular.

The museum was co-founded by Theodore Roosevelt Sr. in 1869. Seventy years later, a bronze statue of his son, the twenty-sixth president of the United States, was erected outside the museum, depicting junior on horseback, accompanied by a Native American and an African guide. Roosevelt was as enthusiastic a hunter as Dame Daphne's Great-Uncle Will, both of whom would no doubt have approved of Price's encomium to hunting in *African Adventure*. "It's a proud life, a wonderful life," he gushes, adding, "Who wouldn't want to be a Hunter?"

A few years after Sir Charles Eliot invited Great-Uncle Will to Kenya, Roosevelt set off on a yearlong hunting and scientific expedition (note how the two go hand in hand), during which he and his party bagged lions, rhinoceroses, hippopotami, zebras, giraffes, buffalo, gazelles, and, naturally, elephants. The Smithsonian Institution's archives break down the numbers:

> All told, Roosevelt and his companions killed or trapped over 11,397 animals, from insects and moles to hippopotamuses and elephants. These included 512 big game animals, including six rare white rhinos. The expedition consumed 262 of the animals. Tons of salted animals and their skins were shipped to Washington; the quantity was so large that it took years to mount them all, and the Smithsonian was able to share many duplicate animals with other museums.

One of these "other museums" was the American Museum of Natural History, where the animals' bodies were stuffed and mounted. Roosevelt, with typical pugnacity, responded to those critics who wondered how the awardee of the 1906 Nobel Peace Prize could have gone on such an orgy of bloodshed by shifting the blame to the quest for knowledge: "I can be condemned only if the existence of the National Museum, the American Museum of Natural History, and all similar zoological institutions are to be condemned."

Roosevelt's trip, which took him from Mombasa in then British East Africa to the Belgian Congo and up the Nile to Khartoum, may have been atypical at the sheer volume and variety of animals that he and his group killed, ate, or captured, but in attitude and purpose he represented very well that strange axial decade that marked the apex of late Victorian and Edwardian Euro-American dominance, with its combustible mixture of scientific exploration, geopolitical grandstanding, racial theories (the anti-Semitic tract *The Protocols of the Elders of Zion* was forged in Russia in 1903), and what we might term "imperial environmentalism" and Conrad calls in his *Last Essays* "geography militant."

The United States was a relative newcomer on the imperial stage. Although the Monroe Doctrine had declared the entire continent of the Americas to be within the ambit of U.S. national interest, it was only at the turn of the twentieth century that the U.S. began to collect territory beyond the continental landmass itself. In 1898, it annexed Guam and Hawaii, and a year later American Samoa and several atolls in the Pacific Ocean. Roosevelt unreservedly supported the cooked-up war with Spain to "liberate" Cuba and the Philippines, both of which fell under the control of the United States, and in 1905 he appended a corollary to the Monroe Doctrine that claimed for the U.S. a possible policing role for the entire Western Hemisphere.

One reason the U.S. did not enter the Scramble for Africa was that it had spent most of the nineteenth century pursuing its own aggressively expansionist policies as part of its manifest destiny to take over the entire breadth of the continent above the Rio Grande and below the 48th parallel. In pushing toward the Pacific, the U.S. government forced the First Nations to migrate, grabbed their land, and deliberately destroyed their natural resources, such as the buffalo herds upon which many plains micro-nationalities depended for their food, clothing, and cultural traditions. By the end of the first decade of the twentieth century, the tens of millions of buffaloes that had once roamed the plains had been reduced to a few hundred, Native American populations had been subdued, and the reservation/national parks systems that kept both humans and animals contained had been put into place—not least under the auspices of Roosevelt himself.

Roosevelt was typically forthright about the purpose of the march of the United States across the continent. "This continent had to be won," he said in the 1892 Lowell Institute Lecture in Boston, Massachusetts. "We need not waste our time in dealing with any sentimentalist who believes that, on account of any abstract principle, it would have been right to leave this continent to the domain, the hunting ground of squalid savages. It had to be taken by the white race."

How interconnected were genuine scientific inquiry, the missionary zeal of evangelization and imperialism, commercial exploitation, racial theory, and the placing of certain species within a confined space for "their own good" as well as the instruction and amusement of others can be illustrated by the case of a twenty-year-old Congolese Mbuti pygmy named Ota Benga. Benga had been captured when soldiers from Leopold II's notorious Force Publique had slaughtered a number of pygmies, including Benga's wife and two children, and had sold others into slavery within the Congo. According to a 2006 article by Mitch Keller in *The New York Times*, Benga was rescued by Samuel Phillips Verner, who'd been commissioned to acquire pygmies and other Africans for an "anthropology exhibit" at the 1904's World Fair in St. Louis. Keller continues: "There, for the edification of American fairgoers, they and representatives of other aboriginal peoples, like Eskimos, American Indians and Filipino tribesmen, would live in replicas of their traditional dwellings and villages."

Keller's article makes clear that the story was more complicated than simply a demonstration of the racism of the time. The individuals who were taken to the World's Fair from Africa in 1904 all returned to the continent; Ota Benga asked to go back to the U.S. with Samuel Verner; he was then displayed at the Bronx Zoo, where the pygmy (unlike the apes with whom he was housed) was allowed to walk around and seems to have initially enjoyed some of the attention that his presence caused. That attention soon became overwhelming and threatening—in a manner that echoes Orwell's treatment in Burma. Keller writes:

On Sunday, Sept. 16, 40,000 people went to the zoo, and everywhere Ota Benga went that day, *The Times* reported, the crowds pursued him, "howling, jeering and yelling."

The newspaper reported, "Some of them poked him in the ribs, others tripped him up, all laughed at him."

The African-American religious establishment was outraged at Ota Benga's situation. Not only was it demeaning to human dignity that a black man should live among apes but such an exhibition supported a Darwinian, as opposed to Christian, idea that humans were descended from animals in the first place. Benga was released and moved to Lynchburg, Virginia, where, says Keller, "[h]e spent a lot of time in the woods, hunting with bow and arrow, and gathering plants and herbs." In 1916, the American immigrant shot himself through the heart. Why he committed suicide is contested. One theory is that he was depressed that the outbreak of war and a lack of financial resources meant he couldn't return to Africa. Samuel Verner himself believed that Ota Benga found his inability to assimilate too painful for him to continue living.

The story of Ota Benga is an extreme example of the commodification and depersonalization of native peoples that we can see in *Heart of Darkness* and which became the operating principle of Leopold II's Congo. What's shocking is not necessarily that a human being was treated like an animal but *how easily* the Christian mission of rescuing someone from slavery slips into scientific taxonomizing and thence to exhibiting a being for instruction *and* entertainment *and* financial gain, and thence to vilification and ridicule, as though imprisonment and domestication are somehow the personal failings of the formerly free individual, who can then be belittled and attacked without regard to their feelings or personal dignity. In this regard, the collection of human and nonhuman animals in zoos forms a strange but almost inevitable arc from fascination at their unfamiliarity to contempt *because of* their familiarity, from enjoyment at their wildness to profiting from their containment.

Consider Willard Price's John Hunt and his sons, who capture animals for carnivals, circuses, film productions, and zoos—where, in the last case, according to *Safari Adventure*, they'll have "good care and furnish education and entertainment to thousands of spectators." The Hunts hold the animals on a farm outside New York City, where Roger we're told has tamed bucking broncos. Only one person in the trilogy questions the Hunts' profession: a Tutsi chief in *Elephant Adventure* named Mumbo demurs at Roger and Hal's wish to capture an elephant and tells them that Rwenzori range is sacred to the creature. His opinion is effectively invalidated in the boys' eyes when he starts talking about how the taking of the animal would disturb the spirits of the mountains where the elephants live. To the Hunts (and we assume, the young readers), what the chief says is, in manifold ways, mumbo jumbo.

Price is frank about the Hunts' motivation. Hunt *père* tells his sons in *African Adventure* that they can make four times as much cash bringing in a live baby hippo for the Hamburg Zoo as they would by killing an adult animal and selling its head to a museum. Throughout the books, Price supplies the value of the various animals the Hunts have set their sights on: a pair of giraffes would fetch £6000 at the Rio Zoo; Tokyo Zoo pays $50,000 for a white elephant and $10,000 for a baby grey elephant. We're informed that all animal hunters are aware that the Japanese pay the most for wildlife, and that the circus impresario P.T. Barnum once coughed up $200,000 for a white elephant.

At some point, the Hunts' obsession with how much an animal is worth becomes so pointed that Price is forced to provide some context: "One would have thought they were money-mad," he murmurs in *African Adventure*. "They were not—usually. But this kind of money was hardly to be made every day." In *Safari Adventure*, Hal feels a pang of regret at giving up the $10,000 a zoo would pay for an okapi, but because few animals survive the journey to America, he recognizes that he can't take the creature. Price approves of Hal's decision: "The important thing right now was not to capture an animal or two for their father, but to do everything possible to stop the killing of the thousands of animals of East Africa. In the long run that would do more for their business of animal-collecting than anything else they could do."

The warden Mark Crosby makes the same point when he persuades the boys to help him track poachers. Hal politely responds that diminished future business prospects wouldn't be the reason they'd join him. Crosby smiles and says he understands. Price glosses: "The Hunts loved animals. They also loved excitement. Perhaps they loved money too." Uncertain as to what the correct course of action should be, the boys call their father, who tells them to assist Crosby for free because it'll be the biggest and best job they've ever had.

This heavy strain of bottom-line pragmatism alongside the quest for adventure accompanies even Roger's affection for and bonding with wild animals. Instead of burying the dead mother of two leopard cubs whom Roger adopts in *African Adventure*, the Hunts sell or give the mother's skin to the "American Museum in New York." When Roger asks his father whether he can keep the orphaned leopard cubs, John Hunt tells him sternly that because grown leopards don't make good pets, they'll have to go to a zoo "where they can be cared for properly." Wildlife rehabilitation as practiced by Dame Daphne would, we imagine, clearly get in the way of business.

If maintaining the delicate balance between capturing animals and shooting them, between experiencing the non-monetized beauty of the outdoors and making serious cash from selling live creatures, and between caring for the animals you come across and bagging your quota isn't already next to impossible for Price, the author is eager to let the reader know that the Hunts are as good to the animals as they are to their fellow humans. "[John] Hunt was naturally kind to animals," he emphasizes in *African Adventure*, "and no less kind to the human animal." This allows Price to claim that what the Hunts do is entirely humane, even when he's forced by the circumstances to answer what one would assume were awkward, if obvious, questions that his young readers might raise. When the Hunts capture a baby hippo, we're told (somewhat defensively) that the animal won't suffer being away from his mother, family members, and freedom because he's young enough to become used to living in a zoo and not miss Africa. When the Hunts "gather" animals, the creatures are sometimes conveniently glad to come along. Commissioned to get two baboons for a traveling circus, for example, Hal heals a baby baboon to the relief of the mother; both then follow him devotedly into captivity.

The Hunts may be "naturally kind" to humans and animals, but not all the non-villainous characters in the books are quite so charitable. In *Safari Adventure*, Tony the warden rails against human overpopulation: "And the faster we multiply, the faster we push the remaining animals off the planet. We seem to think we own everything. How about our fellow-animals—don't they have any rights?" To argue that animals may have rights independent of human utility is both compelling and subversive, although what either Price or some of his characters might mean by "rights" is effectively delimited by their differing concepts of fellowship among them and other creatures.

Tony and Mark Crosby, for instance, have problems with the Maasai cattle, which are overgrazing the land, moving into the protected wildlife areas, and destroying the habitat: "The Masai have no need for so many cattle—they keep them just to show off," Tony complains. "The same thing is happening in the national parks, even in Tsavo. Herds of bony, scrawny, worthless cattle are driving out the wild life." Such an opinion is shared by Roger Hunt who, somewhat tortuously, claims in *African Adventure* that the tsetse fly is an important feature of the ecosystem because it harms cattle: "The Africans raise millions of cattle and the cattle roam all over the land eating the grass right down to the roots, so that there is nothing left for the wild animals. . . . Of course cattle are good to have, but it's also good to have some places left where the most wonderful animals in all the world have a chance to exist."

Price makes sure in *Safari Adventure* that we learn that the Maasai don't eat the cattle they raise. Yet he's clearly wise to the connection between domesticated livestock and the environmental devastation they can cause because of their tendency to overgraze their pasture or destroy riparian habitat. But to say that we shouldn't rear them so they wouldn't decimate the landscape, or we shouldn't eat them so we can be "naturally kind" to these non-wild kinds of animals as well, are steps too far. The Hunts enjoy their breakfasts of bacon and eggs, and John Hunt informs his sons that hyenas are important cleaning mechanisms for the plains, in that they eat dead bodies just as humans do. In his own way, Mark Crosby affirms such a world-view in *Safari Adventure*. Humans are similar to lions, he says: "Nature made them meat eaters—like you and me. They are no more cruel than you and I are when we eat a beefsteak."

The greatest challenge to Price's parsing of appropriate and inappropriate uses of animals, however, is that the Hunts' profession is, in essence, little different from poaching. At the beginning of *Safari Adventure* Price clearly feels the need to suggest a definition: "What is a poacher? In Africa it means a thief who kills animals without a licence and sells the tusks, horns, or other valuable parts." Note how this summary implies that killing *with* a license is legal and thus not poaching (which allows the white hunters and safari operators to continue with their business); that killing any animal *outside* of Africa without a license is acceptable because that's what your average hunter does; and that the pilfering that's taking place is of the valuable parts of the animal and not the stealing of the entire animal from its life on the continent.

Such distinctions can't get around the fact that the Hunts and the poachers are removing wild animals, with little awareness it seems of the effect of that abstraction on the ecosystem or family groups, and are paid very good money by foreign entities to do so. In fact, at one point in *Elephant Adventure* Hal admits of a moral equivalence when he peevishly complains that the Arab sheikh, who plans to sell the white elephant they're both hunting to the King of Siam, has the nerve to be tracking "our" elephant.

Price leaps through numerous hoops in order to differentiate the Hunts from the villains. So plentiful are the animals who arrive at a watering hole in *African Adventure* that it seems to young Roger as if the world's zoos had released their animals. It's a suggestive thought (what if the zoos of the world *did* release their animals back into the wild?) that almost seems to break through the consciousnesses of the other characters. Indeed, although Price periodically issues dire warnings about the condition of African wildlife, John Hunt observes complacently that while "you often read nowadays that wildlife is disappearing, and it's true in a way . . . you can see that there's a lot of it left." (One hears an echo of the French logger whom Prof encountered in the Congo.)

*   *   *

The various gradations of attitude toward animals shown by Price—of which creatures may be taken, which not, by whom, and for what purpose—may seem quaint and old-fashioned, and yet they possess an enduring currency. There are still plenty of companies offering would-be Great White Hunters the chance to bag a large African animal—conveniently rounded up for you by obliging trackers—for a handsome sum. And it's not only fauna who are in danger. As Mia and I worked with Wangari Maathai on *The Challenge for Africa*, an incident in Kenya crystallized the continuing and highly charged complexities surrounding the private ownership of land, class, race, and our relationship with animals.

In 2006, a Kenyan citizen by the name of Thomas Cholmondeley (pronounced "Chumley") was arrested and charged with the murder of another Kenyan citizen, Robert Njoya, who was alleged to have been poaching animals on Cholmondeley's property. This was the second such incident that Cholmondeley had been involved in. The previous year, he'd been acquitted of the murder of a Kenya Wildlife Service employee, Samson ole Sisina, in mysterious circumstances. Cholmondeley claimed he'd been acting in self-defense because he thought the ranger was a robber. In the second case, Cholmondeley was convicted of manslaughter, sentenced to eight months in prison, and released after five.

The crime drew a great deal of attention in Kenya because Cholmondeley was the great-grandson of Lord Delamere (1870–1931), who'd been one of the leading landowners and political figures in the British colonization of Kenya in the first decades of the twentieth century. During that time, vast stretches of land had been set aside for private ownership that were much bigger than the holdings of ordinary settlers such as Prof's father's employer, Mr. Neylan, or Dame Daphne's relatives. African Kenyans and their livestock were largely excluded from these estates, and this remained true beyond independence.

Since the mid-1980s, when hunting wild animals had been banned in the country—ironically under the aegis of Daniel arap Moi, who although no friend of the human elephant Wangari Maathai, was a somewhat late-coming friend of the four-legged kind—these lands had become wildlife preserves, where relatively wealthy white men and women could come to take photographs of the same wild animals that their countryfolk some half a century earlier would have "taken" in a different sense. Fences and patrols circled the area attempting to stop poor Africans from grazing their livestock or farming on the fertile land, or killing the same species that had, literally, been fair game a few decades before.

Through his family, Cholmondeley owns the Soysambu

Ranch and maintains its conservancy for cattle ranching, agriculture, and tourism. That Cholmondeley should have been acquitted of all charges regarding the death of Samson ole Sisina and only convicted of manslaughter for the second killing was, for some Kenyans, proof that almost half a century after independence, one law in Kenya existed for white, influential, aristocratic landowners and another for citizens who weren't any or all of the above.

We asked Prof what she thought about the case (at the time, Cholmondeley was awaiting trial on the second murder charge). In her typically nuanced analysis, she concentrated not on Cholmondeley's motivations and attitudes toward black Africans, of which she had no first-hand knowledge, but on the realities facing Samson ole Sisina and, in particular, Thomas Njoya. She noted that the vast acreages held under private ownership in Kenya placed great pressure on public land, particularly in productive areas, to provide ample food and income, which meant that poaching wildlife on nearby private estates was virtually inevitable. Whereas in Lord Delamere's day the land had been privatized and enclosed partly so that the wealthy could kill wild animals, Soysambu Ranch's protected wild animals from being hunted. In spite of the reversal in attitudes toward wildlife among the elite, the visitors to Soysambu Ranch were, Prof assumed, still mainly neither Kenyan nor, indeed, black African.

Indeed, she added, black Africans like Thomas Njoya saw little of the considerable income generated by foreigners coming to Africa to watch wild animals. Wild animals, instead, might be seen as competitors with live-stock for grazing land, income from the bushmeat trade, or nuisances that trampled crops and threatened home-steads. The solution, as she saw it, was for a more equitable distribution of revenues within the tourism industry and encouragement from the government to enable people like Thomas Njoya to establish businesses on the periph-eries. If, Prof reflected, Thomas Njoya had been provided with investment to enable him to sell tourist mementoes or drinks then he might have been able to buy his food rather than risk his life trying to steal it.

Prof knew this was a challenging proposition. She once wryly commented to us that many visitors to Kenya appeared to express little interest in the human popula-tion of her country, something she considered not merely another facet of the strange and complex relationship between the native peoples of sub-Saharan Africa and those who arrived on its shores, but of the failure of the Kenyan people and its government to develop addi-tional attractions other than the National Parks and the beaches of Mombasa. Prof wasn't surprised that many of the Kenyan schoolchildren who arrived each morning at the David Sheldrick Wildlife Trust to see the orphaned animals being fed and playing were meeting these crea-tures, who were (relatively speaking) in their own back-yard, for the first time. That alienation indicated just how removed so many young and old had become from the natural world and its gifts—whether through urbaniza-tion or enforced displacement—and how imaginatively impoverished they were about how they might change their economic situation.

As a further example of that lack of connection, Prof related to us how, when she was a Member of Parliament, she'd received a phone call at six o'clock in the morning to let her know that three elephants had been seen wandering around her constituency and that people were scared. Her constituency abutted a verdant corridor that elephants walked between Mount Kenya and the Aberdare Range. People had moved into these forested areas, she said, and in order to avoid them the elephants had begun to stray from their normal routes. These three animals had traveled all night and had moved into Mathare, close to Nyeri, at dawn.

Prof telephoned the Kenya Wildlife Service (KWS), who told her that if the people didn't touch or make a noise around the elephants they would move on, but that if the elephants became agitated or confused they would attack. Unfortunately, when the people woke up to find elephants wandering around, they started yelling and beating cooking pots to frighten them off. This only had the effect of disorientating the animals even more, so that they began to head toward the town of Nyeri. To her distress, Prof continued, KWS took the decision to kill the elephants—apparently because they didn't have tranquilizers to sedate them or the means to transport them to a safe area. "I felt very bad about those elephants," she added. After the incident, she said, she'd talked with members of the humane community about establishing a center in her constituency to help train people who would deal with the animals appropriately, but she was voted out of office before she was able to set it up.

Prof hadn't seen an elephant when she was a child. However, it was a matter of some pride to her that she'd been taught not to fear wild animals and to leave them alone, recognizing that mutual respect and caution would enable both human and nonhuman animals to survive. In *Unbowed*, she remembered how her mother had told her that if she ran into a leopard in the forest she should tell it that she was a friend (*wa-ngari* can mean "of the leopard" in Kikuyu). Prof told Mia and me that she often saw antelopes, monkeys, and other animals as a child. She was at pains to inform us, two vegans, that the original Kikuyu diet consisted mainly of vegetables, only supplemented with goat meat during festivals. In *The Challenge for Africa*, she recounted how Kikuyus didn't hunt wild animals, although they were abundant, and that her mother had told her that the rivers of her youth teemed with fish, which the Kikuyu neither killed nor ate. Prof lamented that loss of connection with the natural world—not merely for the delight it had brought to her when she was young but on behalf of the animals themselves, who were victims like the three elephants of our fear of and ignorance about them.

Prof always argued that wild animals had as much right to be on this planet as we did, and that they had an intrinsic value independent of their utility to us. She understood the arguments about overgrazing that Tony the warden offers in *Safari Adventure* (although she wouldn't have been so insulting!). She didn't think Kenyans should rush pell-mell into the consumption of American fast-food in the way that they'd done a century ago in adopting so much high-fat, salty, and oily British and Indian food and drink as their own. She thought it an absurd and tragic paradox that tourists might visit Nairobi National Park in the morning and thrill at the sight of a warthog only to eat his cousin at a game restaurant that evening. It was a travesty that some Kenyans might never have *seen* let alone eaten a member of that species!

Yet, like Willard Price's characters and so many conservationists, Prof made a distinction between domesticated livestock and wild animals by eating the former and advocating for the latter. She didn't ask us more about our diet and we didn't challenge hers. In so doing, we continued to police that perennial divide between those of our fellow animals whom we consider worth preserving and protecting and those whom we consider tasty and unworthy of life beyond our plate. Perhaps the three of us maintained a necessary pact of silence so as not to erect yet another cultural barrier between us. I've no good answer beyond the useful self-protections of silence why, in spite of two decades of championing veganism and animals rights (see my book *The Polar Bear in the Zoo*), I didn't press the issue either with her or with the organizers of the soirée in the American Museum of Natural History, where chickens and shrimp were appetizers but the larger animals were not.

Yet another elephant to add to our herd.

6

Magic Is Unlikely

DURING THE QUESTION-AND-ANSWER session immediately following Daphne Sheldrick's talk at the American Museum of Natural History, in addition to the Kenyan who spoke Kiswahili to Dame Daphne, a middle-aged white man came to the microphone and challenged her belief that the elephants had telepathically communicated the arrival of the vehicle bearing the new orphans. What she had taken for psychic behavior, the man said, was probably the elephants picking up the vibrations of the truck that usually carried the new arrivals to the orphanage.

Dame Daphne responded that hundreds of trucks passed each day along the Nairobi–Mombasa road, so how was it possible for the elephants to know which one was the correct vehicle? The man suggested that the elephants' infrasound capabilities would have detected the specific vibrations of the truck they were used to. Dame Daphne replied that the orphanage had used different trucks through the years, including one that had been especially developed to move three elephants at a time. The man was unconvinced: "Magic is unlikely," he concluded.

As he stepped away from the mike, a considerable number of the audience jeered. Why did some of us so vocally dislike his skepticism? After all, we were in a museum dedicated to the pursuit of science, where one would imagine extrasensory perception, whether human or nonhuman, could be considered, at the least, debatable. Did we—materialistic, rational, twenty-first-century New Yorkers—really believe in magic after all?

As Dame Daphne told the story of her elephants being welcomed by the ex-orphans, I recalled the death two months earlier of Lawrence Anthony, a conservationist based at the Thula Thula game reserve in KwaZulu Natal, South Africa. He was known as "The Elephant Whisperer" because of his skills at rescuing and rehabilitating elephants who'd been deemed "rogue" and had been slated by the authorities to be killed as pests. According to Anthony's son Dylan, twelve hours after his father's death two herds of elephants converged on the conservationist's compound, where they remained for two days. The two herds hadn't visited the house for eighteen months, and it would have taken them twelve hours to make the journey through the bush to the compound. Many of the elephants who made the trek were those whom Anthony had saved from slaughter.

The obvious question is how the elephants knew that Anthony had died. According to Dylan's timeline, the elephants began their journey within an hour of Anthony's death, so it's hard not to conclude that the elephants had some kind of intuition that the whisperer had passed away. How else would they have been informed, especially when you bear in mind that there would have been no vibrations from a truck to indicate his demise? And is it not extraordinary that these two herds arrived at the compound within a few hours of each other? Considering that this story suggests that elephants can plan and coordinate, are conscious, remember, and honor the dead, it's not difficult to see why Dame Daphne would suggest telepathy for the way the elephants could communicate as well.

It's tempting to speculate that one reason why the man was greeted with such disdain was that he simply wasn't responding to what one might call the relational cues of the evening. We weren't at the talk to learn about whether elephants, rhinoceroses, and other animals could or could not do certain things. We wanted to honor their personhood and appreciate their complexity, and to validate our caring about their welfare. The man was not simply deaf to the possibilities of extrasensory perception, he was clueless about the vibrations in the lecture hall!

But why did his statement seem so offensive, beyond the somewhat derisory manner with which he used the word "magic"? In some ways, his skepticism placed him in good company. In 1907, the psychologist Oskar Pfungst had proved that the horse known as Clever Hans hadn't, as was claimed, been calculating the answers to arithmetical problems in his head and tapping them out with his hooves, but had been "reading" physical cues provided unconsciously by his human trainer and the members of the audience who'd asked him the questions. In an article in *The New Yorker*, Burkhard Bilger relates that animals can be trained by "operant conditioning" to perform actions once thought impossible—actions that might be readily mistaken for a sophisticated, reciprocal consciousness. Ken Ramirez, the vice-president of animal training at the Shedd Aquarium in Chicago, tells Bilger: "We have sharks that will swim from tank to tank, and a beluga whale that will present its belly for an ultrasound. Our sea otters hold their eyes open to get drops, and I've had a diabetic baboon submit to regular insulin injections."

The article also relates that recent tests have discovered that, where once it was thought that a dog's nose could detect a few particles per million of a substance, more subtle measuring instruments have now lowered that amount to a few particles per *trillion*. The man questioning Dame Daphne could have concluded, with a degree of humility, that although magic was unlikely as an explanation for how the ex-orphans knew the truck and/or the new elephants were coming, the sensory—let alone emotional and cultural—apparatus of many animals, including the elephant, were obviously currently beyond our calibration: a naturalistic explanation was simply not yet available.

Ever since Thomas Nagel wondered what it would be like to be a bat and concluded that it was impossible to know, other philosophers, as well as cognitive psychologists and ethologists, have attempted to reconcile their commonsense observation that "higher order" animals are not only sentient but clearly possess some sort of interior life and a parallel dearth of scientific instruments capable of ascertaining that mental-sensory *Umwelt* (to use Jakob von Uexküll's term) with the post-Cartesian prejudices that confine complex, self-reflexive thought to *homo sapiens*. Biologist Jonathan Balcombe has written persuasively about how bats inhabit their world, while some philosophers, such as Cora Diamond and Stanley Cavell, have argued that poetry and other forms of literature provide an imaginative way to conceptualize what it might be like to see the world through an animal's eyes.

In her novel *The White Bone*, Barbara Gowdy depicts the interior and exterior lives of a number of elephant families as they attempt to make their way to "The Safe Place," a location free from the poaching that claims the lives of many elephants in the book. Gowdy imagines an elephant *Weltanschauung* that is as intensely felt and smelled as it is seen and heard. It's a world of deep bonds within families, of moments of ecstatic madness when female and male are in estrus or musth respectively. Some elephants possess a third eye, a capacity to mind-read and prophesy that shifts from creature to creature, depending on seniority within the family group. It's a gift that causes the animal's skull to enlarge and the creature falls into a kind of dreamtime that links the past with the future.

In Gowdy's inspired engagement, the elephants' world

is dominated by memories, which tie communities and families together and sometimes overwhelm individuals because they *cannot* forget. It's a feature of their intelligence that they're not only capable of empathy, planning, and reason but that they're also superstitious (their belief in the white bone's talismanic power is, in some cases, tragically misplaced) and spiritually invested in cosmology, rituals, and prayers (admittedly, the least convincing aspects of Gowdy's vision). Each elephant has a singular personality and favorite and least favorite relatives. Some are fantasists and others are pragmatists; some are cautious and others intemperate.

For her research, Gowdy read many books about elephants by naturalists and animal protectionists and visited the Mara to see the animals in situ. Although the author wouldn't claim that her book is "scientific" in a manner that might satisfy the gentleman who expressed his doubts to Dame Daphne that night at the museum, *The White Bone* offers to our sympathetic imagination a picture of an elephantine universe at once familiar and yet beyond our ken, precisely because these animals' *Umwelt* is so much more concentrated and intensely sensuous than ours that it appears supernatural to us. Indeed, to all intents and purposes, the elephants' physical, psychic, and affective experience is magical because to us it's literally inconceivable.

Even if the gentleman had responded in the way I suggested above, there's no guarantee he would have met with any more understanding a reception, if only because the exchange among the audience, the man, and Dame Daphne wasn't only about ESP in elephants. The audience that night was overwhelmingly female, as were the great majority of the questioners, including a series of ever younger and more diminutive girls, who wanted to know about Dame Daphne's life with the animals. What was it like to see an orphaned elephant come in to the shelter? Was she ever scared about her safety with the animals around her? Could she describe her typical day? Did the elephant keepers live on the grounds since they slept with the elephants? When did she first know she loved elephants? Did the humans make the elephants sick?

It's my bet that, perhaps unwittingly, the man's observation triggered a particular association. Through Dame Daphne's extensive experience watching and living with the animals in their environment; in her naming them and responding to them and their young as they spanned the generations; in her emotional connection to them and her humility in the face of what these animals had gone through; and in her advocacy on behalf of the creatures as their habitat was threatened and they were abused by human beings, this white woman of a certain age may have evoked for the audience another female of British heritage who'd studied animals in Africa and had been knighted: Dr. Jane Goodall.

Goodall's study of wild chimpanzees in Gombe, Tanzania, had been initially criticized in the 1960s by an overwhelmingly male scientific community for breaking the protocols that required animals to be given numbers and not names; for not studying them under controlled conditions, perhaps in a laboratory; and for the cardinal sin of anthropomorphism (the assigning of supposedly solely human characteristics, such as an individual personality or thought processes, to nonhuman animals). Jane Goodall is one of several women who challenged the notion of what it means to be an ethologist. Biruté Galdikas with orangutans in Indonesia, Dian Fossey with gorillas in Rwanda (both, like Goodall, encouraged in their work by another scientist familiar to us—Louis Leakey), and Patricia Wright with lemurs in Madagascar have contested the idea that an animal, especially social primates like ourselves, can be truly understood outside of their natural environment, or that we ensure greater methodological rigor by cutting off comprehension of our *own* behavioral patterns for fear of assigning them to the animal. By questioning Dame Daphne's observation of the paranormal, was the man in effect suggesting that women don't think scientifically? And was the audience, in its robust demurral, arguing that their issue wasn't that Dame Daphne wasn't being scientific enough; it was that the man's notional spectrum of possible knowledge was too narrow?

Perhaps the audience was hypersensitive because, like the first critics of Jane Goodall's work, the man was in effect challenging Dame Daphne's academic qualifications. (Goodall hadn't received a degree when she began her studies; Dame Daphne never went to university and was awarded an honorary doctorate for her discovery that coconut milk could be used to nurse infant elephants.)

Although she was highly credentialed as a scientist, Wangari Maathai likewise confronted sexism at the outset of her academic career at the University of Nairobi. In the early days of the Green Belt Movement, the professional (male) foresters condescended to the rural women and questioned their ability. You need a diploma to plant a tree and look after it, they said to her and the women. Prof didn't think it was that hard. She told the women that they should use their "woman sense": they were always planting seeds in the ground and tending them. If they nurtured the seedling, watered it, and made sure the goats didn't eat it, it would grow. "The good ones germinated and the bad ones didn't," she writes in *Unbowed*, "and the ones that did looked exactly like the trees planted by the foresters. . . . These women were our 'foresters without diplomas'" (136).

It was typical of Prof that she should, in public at least, trumpet unlettered common sense based on practical experience as much as, if not more than, academic study and diploma-based rank-pulling. She knew what she knew and had experienced and didn't need a piece of paper or letters after her name to buttress her ideas. The numerous honorary doctorates and awards she received were only ever important to her in that they burnished her international profile, which protected her politically in Kenya, enabled her to raise funds for the Green Belt Movement, and offered an official imprimatur for the grassroots, bottom-up approach to community development that she championed.

It's perhaps unfair to freight the man's response of "magic is unlikely" with more portent than it can carry, but it's hard not to discern in his curt formulation and the hostility of the audience not only resistance to his belief about what is or isn't "science" but an instinctive reaction to another embedded association: that of women with magic and superstition, especially when it comes to animals. In the European Middle Ages, it was believed that single or singular women of mature years were connected to dark forces—echoes of which continue today in the folkloric iconography of witches on broomsticks wearing pointed hats, and associating themselves with the black arts and black animals (ravens, cats, etc.). They were gossips, spreaders of "old wives' tales," as though women with no formal employment and/or education are destabilizing forces and disseminators of unverifiable, anecdotal, or false information. Women's connection with and closeness to certain species of animals were both cause and effect of their irrationality, unreliability, and rebelliousness.

The social historian Carolyn Merchant and ecofeminist scholars such as Barbara Noske, Marti Kheel, Greta Gaard, and Carol J. Adams have demonstrated that the desacralization and dis-integration of the natural world and accompanying scientific and mercantile-industrial endeavors that took place from the sixteenth century onward in Europe were frequently described using sexual tropes . . . and that they still are in the West. Nature (always feminine) is recalcitrant and disobedient, unwilling to reveal her secrets unless she—and the creatures she births—are forcibly restrained, penetrated, eviscerated, and their (re)production controlled.

As we've already noted, men in power criticized Wangari Maathai because she'd divorced her husband, mobilized other women, and spoke out against injustice. To these men, she was untamed and outside the bounds of respectable behavior. She needed, said one Member of Parliament, to be circumcised (both a literal and metaphorical cutting down to size of her sex) to bring her under control. In the attacks on Prof and the women of the Green Belt Movement, we can hear echoes of the age-old assault on older women and traditional healers who—like Artemis in the forest, surrounded by animals and other women and hidden from the gaze of men—place themselves beyond the determining hands or wedding bands of those who wish to strip the land of assets and assign themselves the rights to use what grows on top or within it as they see fit. Although Prof would almost certainly have expressed caution about my associative thinking above, it's surely evocative that she not only placed herself in solidarity with all groups looking to protect the land from unplanned and inequitable development but in Nairobi in 1981 marched with members of the Chipko movement—women who hugged trees that were slated to be bulldozed—to urge the conservation and defense of forests.

It's not too far-fetched therefore to see her effectively embracing an identity that joined the protection of sacred groves with women's individual *and* collective selves in opposition to a similarly deeply intertwined set of ideas about who a scientist is and what remains the appropriate way to conduct science, who should have rights to the land and for what purpose, and who is best equipped to engage with and tame the "wild." Through nonviolent civil disobedience in concert with tree-planting campaigns in "illegal" areas, or in sit-ins with women in Uhuru Park and in the crypt of All Saints Cathedral in downtown Nairobi, Prof contrasted herself with the cult of masculinity that has long associated itself with the "harvesting" of trees and wild animals, the manly life of the outdoorsman, the supposedly disinterested pursuit of wholly extractive scientific knowledge, and the generating of pecuniary wealth at the expense of the commonweal.

*   *   *

For boys such as myself, raised on adventure stories from the middle years of the last century, it was clear how I should conduct myself once I set myself free from the constraining, emasculating comforts of hearth and home. When John Hunt, a kindly although remote figure, is conveniently injured with a bad back in *African Adventure*, his two sons continue the work undaunted. The father's absence not only usefully allows Price to demonstrate the boys' bravery and resourcefulness but the boys can show their dad (and Roger his older brother) that they're worthy of his respect and love because they don't need him. The boys' self-perception as solo operators means that those who do assist them (including their thirty Afri can employees) are essentially invisible, even though the tasks they're set require collaboration, trust, and interpersonal communication—skills and qualities one might also imagine would be important for successful teamwork. These ideas, however, run counter to the notion that the brothers have to think for themselves, on their feet, and take personal risks to achieve their goals.

The rites of passage that Hal and Roger's escapades pastiche (for instance, the capturing of a dangerous animal proves that one is a warrior) naturally require women to be entirely absent: the boys don't seem to miss their home and no mother is mentioned, remembered, or mourned. The boys don't appear to notice African women; and Hal—although the same age as my father when he stopped off in Durban on his way to India, hormones coursing through his body—seems never to allow them into his thoughts. True, there is Zulu, the faithful hound of Mali, one of the African team, but Price assures us in *African Adventure* that "[t]hough a female, the dog was every bit as strong, courageous and beautiful as a male." So much like a male is she, indeed, that by *Safari Adventure* she's changed sex.

The notion that trade and work in the bush are not suitable for *respectable* women—indeed, that the dirty businesses of making a killing of any sort are men's domains—is not merely echoed in the virility (*vir* is Latin for "man") of the settlers lauded in *Kenya: Britain's Most Attractive Colony*, but reinforced in *Heart of Darkness*. "Girl! What? Did I mention a girl?" exclaims Marlow. "Oh, she is out of it—completely. They—the women I mean—are out of it—should be out of it. We must help them to stay in that beautiful world of their own, lest ours gets worse" (69). The Intended's ethereal disconnection from the horrific and corrupting world that Kurtz inhabits is reinforced when Marlow visits her. She seems as spectral as her fiancé, "floating towards" him in the dusk (106), "a tragic and familiar Shade" (110).

In that moment, Marlow is reminded of Kurtz's African concubine. She in turn is as elaborately decked out as the Intended, and in her own way as expensive to maintain: she wears "bizarre things, charms, gifts of witch-men, that hung about her, glittered and trembled at every step. She must have had the value of several elephant tusks upon her" (87). How interesting that this ebony woman—both a contrasting figure with the pale Intended and, like the European, occluded by her accouterments—should be measured in the same way that Kurtz has valued his entire venture in Africa: through the acquisition and economic valuation of ivory—even the "black ivory" of slavery mentioned in *Kenya: Britain's Most Attractive Colony*! And note how the black woman is literally animalized, spiritualized, and dehumanized by what she wears upon her: she embodies magic, the forest, and the feral. Is it enough of a link between the appropriation and valuation of the Intended and Kurtz's African princess that the former is discovered by Marlow in a room where a grand piano stands "massively in a corner" (106)—its keys made of ebony hardwood and ivory? Are not both of them the ultimate baubles of the Great White Hunter—the wealthy man who trades in slaughter and owns and disowns women—to play with at his leisure?

It's consistent with Marlow's visualization of the native woman as a fetishized and valuable object that he should also view the continent (in a theme we've already encountered) as a giant womb, the loamy dark matrix that is both Mother Earth and Mama Africa: "the colossal body of the fecund and mysterious life seemed to look at her, pensive, as though it had been looking at the image of its own tenebrous and passionate soul" (87). The various futile efforts of the men forcibly to penetrate the forest and snatch their riches take on sexual characteristics. They are part endeavor to tame the uncontrolled virgin territory, strip her of the shadows that hide her nakedness, and clothe her in civilization; and part rapine and subjugation to extract her riches and harness her enseeded, timeless energy for their own raddled bodies. The forest draws the men in by a fatal power that must be co-opted if they are to retain their potency, fulfill their fantasies, and acquire their wealth. The Kenyan politicians who criticized Prof for being "un-African" and demanded that she be circumcised were drawing on this heady idea of a woman, like the land and the forest, needing to be tamed and cut, lest its impudent sexuality overrun the male outposts of progress. Here, the desire to control the feminine reaches across the century to trump colonial, post-colonial, and racial identities.

To turn to *Love, Life, and Elephants* from this male nightmare of woman as amorphous, alluring, dark, and destructive or a valuable and vulnerable commodity to be brought under the protective and exploitative hand of man is to discover, as in Wangari Maathai's reconfiguration of the notion of the forest, a completely different conceptualization of the female. Throughout Dame Daphne's book, as the orphans arrive at her home and live and grow surrounded by her nuclear human family, the groupings of other animals, and the larger community of human attendants, we notice how *individual* the animals are (they're all named and possess characters) and yet how embedded they are in relationships—among their own kind and among the various creatures who end up living within the compound. Gowdy, too, depicts her elephants as capable of communicating with other animals, including cheetahs and hyenas who would do them harm, through a kind of telepathic miasma. In *Love, Life, and Elephants*, we see animals constantly moving among families; forming troops, packs, herds, and pairs; and creating friendships and alliances among species. The book illustrates in numerous ways that, *contra* the Hunts, independence is *not* a valuable survival mechanism but potentially fatal instead. Simply put, without others, we'd die.

It's surely a cause and a consequence of Dame Daphne's sense of her animals' personhood and their familial existence that she places no *material* value on those she rescues: it is their survival to adulthood in the environment in which they're meant to live that carries their worth for her. It's as if seeing the animals in the context of a family, troop, or herd makes it impossible to consider them merely replaceable, interchangeable representations of species to be shipped around the world for our amusement. Death in Dame Daphne and Barbara Gowdy's elephant societies is inevitable, sometimes violent, and to be mourned appropriately. But then the family is reconfigured, new connections are forged, and the herd moves on, under the guidance of another female.

In their differing ways, therefore, the work of Daphne Sheldrick and Wangari Maathai stands in opposition to masculinist environmental and political engagement and undermines both. Whereas the *Boy's Own* world of Roosevelt and Price, and the accompanying scientific and economic endeavors, involve the steady subtraction of animate life from the environment so it can be placed in a sterile, ordered milieu of cages and cases, or stuffed and mounted in painted landscapes, or burnt to cinders, trimmed, and felled—and the individual man self-actualizes and appreciates Nature best by removing the *anima* from wild bodies or opening up the forests to valuable extraction—Dame Daphne and Prof take what has been destroyed or damaged and repair and renew it *in place*.

As opposed to Price, who sees value in collecting species virtually willy-nilly and believes that learning and entertainment consist in removing the animal from its location outside to a city, where it sits inside an enclosure or under the big top for our amusement, Dame Daphne's working life has been dedicated to the proposition that wild animals should be set free, that they are not transposable or interchangeable, and that we learn so much from them, and enjoy them more, when they live within the context of their herds and ecosystems. In fact, since her entire book resonates with stories about her own family—human and nonhuman—it's fair to say that Dame Daphne argues that our very animality, our common mammalian heritage, cannot be truly expressed *except* within a social structure that honors connection and the ties that bind us together.

It's also surely no coincidence that so much of Dame Daphne's and Prof's work has involved females—whether working together cooperatively in the Green Belt Movement or in the fostering of young calves by the matriarchs of the elephant herds. That their efforts have continued against enormous odds in a world structured around men's excavation, severance, destruction—the cutting out and cutting off and cutting down of life—is, in its way, a kind of magic: Marlow's "desperate belief" (52) that at some point in the future the craven scrambling for resources and domination might come to an end before the last rhinoceros is killed, the last tusks are sawn off, or the last tree is felled.

*   *   *

In the previous chapter, we discussed the imperial legacy of hunting, the gathering of ivory, and scientific collecting. At the start of her book, Dame Daphne wondered how her relatives could have had such a cavalier attitude toward the taking of wildlife. We also had cause to question that attitude as it was expressed two generations later in Willard Price's books—when the removal was of the living as well as the dead. Unfortunately, as *Love, Life, and Elephants* illustrates so vividly and wrenchingly, the orphans arriving at the Trust remind us that the battle Dame Daphne wages to protect African elephants and rhinoceroses from human predation is never-ending. Despite our greater global awareness of the complexity of these and other animals' lives and the vital importance of conservation, we unfortunately inhabit a world of murderous exploitation of elephants that Willard Price in the 1960s and Charlie Marlow in 1900 would recognize all too well.

Dame Daphne writes that droughts, increasing human population, and poaching reduced Kenya's elephant population by tenfold between 1973 to 1989 (280), and the situation is deteriorating throughout Africa. In an article in *National Geographic,* Bryan Christy cites figures of a continent-wide population of 1.3 million in 1979 and between 472,000 and 690,000 today. He adds that 25,000 elephants were killed in 2011 alone, and this, he observes, might be a considerable underestimation. The decimation continued in 2012. NBC News on March 15, 2012, reported the deaths of 200 elephants in three months in Cameroon (Matthew Scully reports the number as 450), and stated that the elephant population of Virunga National Park in the Democratic Republic of Congo had declined from about 3,000 in 1989 to only 400 today. South Africa lost 400 rhinoceroses to poachers in 2010, while in May 2013, it was reported that a gang had killed a group of forest elephants in Dzanga-Ndoki Park in the Central African Republic.

These poachers are much more sophisticated than Thomas Njoya or Sindar Singh. Jeffrey Gettleman in *The New York Times* suggests that militias such as Congo's Lord's Resistance Army, the al-Shabab of Somalia, and Darfur's janjaweed slaughter the elephants and use the tusk-money to buy arms—as do several criminal syndicates throughout Africa. And it's not only unregulated forces that are, apparently, doing the killing. The death of twenty-two elephants in Garamba National Park in the Democratic Republic of Congo in April 2012 has been blamed on members of the Ugandan military, who gathered ivory worth more than a million dollars.

Daphne Sheldrick doesn't go into detail about the kind of trauma such destruction might have caused these elephants—whether a century ago or today. But, befitting their folkloric memory, and from the evidence of the gentleness and affection with which the orphaned and wild elephants responded to Lawrence Anthony and Dame Daphne and her keepers, it's obvious that elephants can differentiate between humans who'll hurt them and those who won't. Conversely, as Charles Siebert observes in a 2006 article in *The New York Times*, research suggests that "[d]ecades of poaching and culling and habitat loss . . . have so disrupted the intricate web of familial and societal relations by which young elephants have traditionally been raised in the wild, and by which established elephant herds are governed, that what we are now witnessing is nothing less than a precipitous collapse of elephant culture." Indeed, according to a study by Heidi Tingvold of the biology department at the Norwegian University of Science and Technology and Robert Fyumagwa of the Tanzania Wildlife Research Institute, stress levels among elephants are measurably higher outside wildlife preserves, where hunting is allowed, than within them. The authors write: "[T]he reason for the higher [stress] level in the high-risk areas [is] thought to be a result of long-ongoing hunting activity, which has led the animals to associate humans and vehicles with detrimental effects."

Poaching's destruction of these African elephant cultures has been accompanied by the loss of habitat for, exploitation of, and assignment of endangered status to their Asian cousins, who've been subject to domestication for many centuries. Within Asian societies, elephants have been employed as weapons of war and to drag felled trees to be shaped into timber—two endeavors that human beings appear to have found compelling for millennia. Asian elephants are favored for zoos and circuses because they're viewed as more passive and trainable than their African brethren. High rates of human population, urban sprawl, and the intensiveness of agriculture in South and Southeast Asia have led to conflict, with humans and elephants killed as each has moved in search of food into the others' habitat.

Both Bryan Christy and Jeffrey Gettleman, writing in *The New York Times* and commenting on National Public Radio, locate China's increasing wealth as the reason for the apparently insatiable demand for ivory. Christy says that, although China is by far the largest market for ivory, religious artifacts and amulets for Catholics and Buddhists in the Philippines, Thailand, Vietnam, and elsewhere in Southeast Asia are also providing a ready, illegal market, where ivory can fetch anything from a few hundred dollars to $1,500 per piece. Writing in *The New York Times* in January 2012, Bettina Wassener reported that "Hong Kong customs officials in November [2011] seized 33 rhinoceros horns, 758 ivory chopsticks and 127 ivory bracelets, worth about 17.4 million Hong Kong dollars, or $2.2 million, from a container shipped from Cape Town." This is not the worst of it. Wassener wrote nine months later: "The authorities in Hong Kong have intercepted one of the largest shipments of illegal ivory in history—1,209 elephant tusks and ivory ornaments weighing more than 8,400 pounds."

At the American Museum of Natural History, Dame Daphne observed how substantial a problem China's growing affluence and consumption patterns are for elephants (Christy indicates that 90,600 pounds of ivory were seized in China between 1989–2011, which obviously doesn't count the ivory not captured). Indeed, the first question that evening came from a woman who asked if the Sheldrick Trust was undertaking any action or something could be done by the public to "move along . . . into the twenty-first century the mentality of the Asian population" regarding ivory and the medicinal uses of rhinoceros horns. Dame Daphne confirmed the dimensions of the challenge.

She said that the Chinese were very involved in Africa and were facilitating the poaching; that the high price of ivory had made poaching a very attractive proposition to poor Africans; and that corruption made the illegality easier. "The key to controlling the poaching," she continued, "lies in stopping the ivory trade. And as long as ivory's on the market, and the International Convention in Trade in Endangered Species [CITES] has very misguidedly allowed the southern African states to sell their ivory stockpiles [*sic*]. And that has fueled the poaching. Since they've sold the stockpiles in 2008, the poaching is completely out of control throughout Africa now, and it's beyond the capacity of local governments to control it, bearing in mind that there's a lot of corruption there, too, and the temptation to get involved in big money is very big."

The burden, she said, rested with the international community through CITES to ban ivory totally and forever, and not just for a couple of years. It was a race against time. "We all do what we can to limit the damage done in the field," she added, "but we cannot actually influence [the] Chinese government. That has to be the international community." She commented that ivory was perceived in the Far East as a status symbol and the elephant a source of power. The rhinoceros's horn, she said, was seen as a cure-all, but was in fact, merely a large nail. If everyone just bit their fingernails, she added to laughter and applause, they'd receive the same benefits.

No one contested this narrative, but, as we've already seen in our analysis of the Congo Free State, *Kenya: Brit-*

ain's Most Attractive Colony, and Willard Price's works, villainous Oriental meddling in Africa for its own dastardly ends, with only the altruism of the Western powers standing in the way to protect the innocent natives, is an old and reliable trope for the West's justification of its own exploitation of the continent. It's easy to forget that the ivory now carved into religious artifacts, geegaws, and curios in Vietnam and China was once shaped into such essentials as billiard balls and dominoes ("the bones" [6] with which the Accountant on the *Nellie* is toying architecturally at the start of *Heart of Darkness*), as well as the Intended's piano keys. The consumer base may have shifted from Europe and North America to the Far East, but the impulse of extraction and the desire to show off one's wealth through the killing of the animal, or the mounting and stuffing of it, remain universal.

For Wangari Maathai, China's presence in Africa was merely another cycle in the ever-turning wheel of non-African powers wanting the continent's natural resources and promising development, employment, and riches to the native peoples in exchange for unfettered access to them. What perturbed her was that, as far as she was concerned, African leaders were still all too willing to give away their citizens' birthrights for a pittance; and too eager to allow non-natives (such as the Vietnamese in the kilns in the Congo forest) to do the work, and thereby continue to stymie attempts to build skills and capacity in African countries. That no one was willing to say "no" to China, she thought, merely showed how the

Great Power dynamic that once defined the relationship between Europe and Africa had shifted eastward.

A larger point, however, needs to be made than who is to blame for endangering which species. Although our collective *scientific* knowledge about the role that elephants, rhinoceroses, and other large animals play in their ecosystems is greater now than it was a century ago, beneath the veneer of conventions, beyond the rhetoric of sustainable use and viable animal populations, and woven into the struggles of East versus West, a strange and bloody thread binds all these activities together—one perhaps we've never fully come to terms with.

Whether it's the bushmeat trade, which supplies the restaurants of middle-class, urbanized Africans throughout the continent and in the Diaspora; or the wild game restaurants near national parks throughout southern Africa that satisfy the curiosity of the tourists who'd express little interest in eating crocodile, warthog, or snake in any other venue—whether we're from London, Lagos, San Francisco, or Beijing; or whether it's the trade in ivory and rhinoceros horn and other exotic species . . . it's clear that the acquisition of the animal body continues to exert its totemic fascination on us, as a symbol of cultural and culinary atavism, a repository of a hypermasculinity marked by conquest and sexual prowess, or as a connection to the spirits of our ancestors and the worlds beyond our own.

It's an old, old story. In our continued decimation of wildlife from East to West, we hear the reverberation of Gilgamesh's fear that unless he can truly tame Nature—

unless he can harness the wildness that exists beyond his city walls—he hasn't fully captured the power of being alive. Willard Price inadvertently touches on this paradox when Mark Crosby calls the African landscape "the world's biggest zoo." Price knows that it's precisely because Africa is *not* thought of as a zoo—that the animals don't exist at the behest of men, in a setting for which they are wholly adapted—that this landscape holds such appeal for us. So attractive is it, in fact, that we have to obliterate it or tame it, because to leave it alone would be to deny both our being drawn to it and our wish to stamp our identities upon it.

And this is one of the great ironies—one that links Marlow's worldview with that of Dame Daphne's: one effect of the "civilizing project" in Africa from the mid-nineteenth century until today has been to turn Willard Price's grandiose idea of a global zoo into a fact. As free as the wildlife in the national parks may appear, they're hemmed in on every side by human barriers, whether cities or fences or the threat of being killed as pests or unwelcome predators. As in a zoo, the animals are sometimes moved for breeding purposes or culled when they become too numerous in one area. The "Big Five" (buffalo, leopard, elephant, lion, and rhinoceros) that used to be harassed and hunted in Africa until they were shot are now harassed and hunted by convoys of tourist vehicles until a satisfactory number of camera shots have been taken. In fact, by calling these places "parks" or "reserves" we're implicitly acknowledging their artificiality. They are now sites of entertainment or leisure, open-air repositories of clusters of desirable animals, ready to be shaped for so-called species health or cut back so they're not a nuisance—often to the domesticated animals whom we eat and who've taken over their land. Animals in these places are now expected to "pay their way," if they're going to survive.

Wild animals aren't the only beings whose lives have been curtailed and fenced in by outside forces. Like Ota Benga in the Bronx Zoo, the peoples of the African continent have for centuries been subjected to restrictions on their movements as human beings. They, too, were captured and transported for our labor, our entertainment, and (during slavery) the prodding humiliation and violence of our bored, idle hands. From the slave trades of the Atlantic and Indian oceans to the reservation system established by the British in Kenya (whether the camps during the Mau Mau insurgency or the areas for the white settlers) where certain animals and humans were included and others excluded, habitats for humans and animals have been contested, with a powerful minority often determining where the less powerful majority are allowed to exist, if not quite live.

Wangari Maathai notes in *The Challenge for Africa* that the African peoples have been subject to so much cultural destruction, destabilization, and deracination that it's hardly surprising that they may be suffering from post-traumatic stress disorder, and at times acting out much in the same way as the elephants whose families have been disrupted, their bodies exploited, and their habitat destroyed. If they return to "magical" beliefs that sustained them in the past—no matter how perverse or self-defeating—it's partly because for at least a century the project of "civilization" (Kurtz's great endeavor, mired in the hypocrisy of its own savagery) has failed so spectacularly to provide them with security, collective purpose, self-identity, and spiritual fulfillment. When the human and nonhuman residents of the continent try to escape to "The Safe Place" where they're less at risk of death or exploitation, the rest of the world works hard to keep them on the other side of the walls that form our various gated communities—whether Europe or America or whatever settlement we've established in the bush or in the city where we can observe them when it suits us. How interesting and inspiring we find these beings, as long as we can observe their exotic, "stereotypical" behavior from a safe distance, and intrude upon them to extract what it is we want from them and corral them on our own terms!

But let us turn away from the dark magic of Africa toward our own. When you examine the reasons why the animals are being killed—a belief in their aphrodisiacal properties; the amulets and knickknacks promising you luck, blessings, children, protection from the evil eye, the hope that they may stave off disease or death (or even plain ornamentation); that killing and/or eating an animal (whether domesticated or wild) makes you a man or brave or strong or fertile; the transubstantiation of creaturely vitality through its flesh into your body—you realize that our planet, nearly five thousand years removed from that of the King of Uruk, is filled with all kinds of mumbo jumbo about these creatures, stemming from Marlow's "desperate belief" that our inevitable passing away can be delayed if we just harnessed the animal spirits and organized and controlled Nature that little bit more. For all her belief in homeopathy and telepathy, Daphne Sheldrick was the most rational person in the room that night. For, ultimately, although Rumi's parable should warn us about the limits of finding the essential Elephant, at least Dame Daphne allowed these animals to present themselves as they *were* over years and not what they represented to those who prodded and snatched at these creatures and literally took them apart as their passport to happiness, to heaven, or to wealth beyond measure.

In fact, we might speculate that when the superstitious chief who believes that eating a leopard's heart might cure him tells Hal Hunt that the boy may have to learn some things as well as teach them, is he half-hinting that his own belief in the animating powers of the ingested animal may be as unfounded as Hal's idea that the body of the leopard he takes to the zoo might miraculously ease the ache in his heart for authentic masculinity, or immortality, or the replenishment of our inevitably waning powers? Is he telling the boy, *You, too, crave the enchantment of a connection with the other-than-human world—one so profound that it cures any fever?*

But for all that Hal might wish it so, magic is unlikely.

7

Out There

APPENDED TO OR annexed by, or standing as the *antithesis* to the *thesis* that is the American Museum of Natural History, the Frederick Phineas and Sandra Priest Rose Center for Earth and Space depicts the origins, size, and dimensions of the exterior and interior universes of the cosmos and the human. The scale models and circular walkways that allow us to wind backward and forward through the fourteen billion years of the universe's existence remind us not only how much time elapsed following the Big Bang without any cellular form in evidence, but how vast is the "out there" where life hasn't yet been observed, and how much remains to be discovered. It only takes a few moments in the planetarium for one to realize not only how extremely improbable it was that this rock we call home should shelter life, but how very likely it is that life of some kind exists elsewhere in the universe.

The planetarium's expansive representations of space and time communicate certain conundrums. It's possible that, unless we destroy the ecosystems upon which human life depends, by the time that Earth has ceased to be habitable for humans within the next 500 million years, we'll have found a way to colonize space. Or, since millions of years yet remain for our species to evolve, we (whoever "we" turn out to be) may have become beings that possess the ability to survive in much warmer climatic conditions, with greater concentrations of carbon dioxide, methane, and nitrous oxide in the atmosphere and much reduced biodiversity, allowing us to buy a few more precious millennia to find another planet on which to live.

Yet, how are we to conceive of a future when it's so hard to imagine a past without *any* human presence—as the history of the universe has almost entirely consisted of? How can we hypothesize what our world will look like a century or even a millennium ahead, let alone one as far distant from us today as the arrival of the species *homo sapiens* was from the twenty-first century? Would there be anything to recognize at all, or would we have been superseded in the way *homo erectus*, *homo Neanderthalensis*, or *homo ergaster* were?

More poignantly or disturbingly perhaps, who knows how the other animals that surround us now might evolve? *Homo sapiens* is only one of four thousand known mammalian species among the perhaps two to three million animal species we've identified. Although we count ourselves successful as a species, our numbers and variety are dwarfed by the 850,000 different insect species and 500,000 species of nematodes that scientists have enumerated, and about which cosmologist Brian Swimme tells us in *The Universe Story* (139–140). Who are we to say that in ten million years, a variety of insect, parasite, or worm might not have taken our place as the anxious reflector of the universe's continual expansion? For why should that self-knowledge only be limited to ourselves? After all, the couple of hundred thousand years that *homo sapiens* has been in existence is too short a time for any major biological change to have manifested itself. In sum, we've no means of imagining a past or a future without us, and yet vast stretches of both have been and probably will be devoid of human presence and human thought.

We might choose to believe that the universe continues to unfold in an ever more complex process of increasing levels of awareness, and that some sort of honor is shouldered by being burdened with those higher faculties within the empty cold of space. We might agree with Brian Swimme that, given that the universe contains everything there is or has ever been, such extraordinary vehicles for awareness as the ear and eye didn't develop within carbon-based life-forms only so creatures could negotiate their way through life more adeptly, but that the universe itself developed the eye and ear in order to *know* itself better and will itself into consciousness. Perhaps more refined senses will emerge to unlock the secrets of the cosmos, and whatever beings appear in the future will cast off the decay of our flawed bodies. Perhaps they'll possess minds that reach beyond even the furthest horizons of our imagination, and that what is mysterious to us now will become evident to them.

Such unanswerable questions emerge naturally from the Rose Planetarium. However, the Anne and Bernard Spitzer Hall of Human Origins in the museum stimulates other, less exalted reactions. The hall displays a video in which a number of scientists talk about how the theory of evolution and their personal spiritual, religious, and philosophical beliefs mesh contentedly one with the other: the former being the theory of how we became who we are; the latter attempting to answer why. The video demonstrates the museum's defensive humility, which suits our less certain age (and the agitated antagonism of Creationists) rather than the confidence of a century earlier, when, as we've seen throughout this book, the march of Civilization, Progress, and Science seemed assured enough that a museum could be built to house them all and, as the Holocaust began in Europe, a statue of the blustering optimist, American exceptionalist, and great conservationist could be placed outside it, straddling an animal and leading the savages into the White Man's Future.

This side-by-side arrangement of the purviews of science and the responsibilities of philosophy and religion was, for me, too comfortable and tidy. No matter how admirable the range and number of our scientific discoveries, our harnessing of the planet's natural resources, and the refinements of our self-consciousness—let alone the awesomeness of our God and the promises made by our saviors—we delude ourselves if we don't recognize that all human experience, let alone our individual lifespans, are but a blip, and that what we take to be the unique gifts and brilliance of humankind *may* simply be the transitory extensions of one primate species outrun by time, our own shortsightedness, and delusions of specialness encouraged by our overly analytical brain.

Walking through the Spitzer hall, one is struck by what I imagine is an unintended consequence of giving our species' ancestors their own rooms. As one strolls amid the dioramas displaying our offshoots going about their business on the savannah in various states of hairiness and undress, it's impossible not to notice how diminished, furtive, and hunkered down we appear. Battling dinosaurs loom above you in the hall when you enter the museum from Central Park West; a life-sized replica of a blue whale hangs above the hall filled with other cetaceans and sharks; even the bones of the proboscideans possess an ossified majesty. Yet there we are, the nervous, hunched-over hominid *variora*: scanning the horizon for predators, huddled around a campfire, hatching plans to enact our revenge on a world and its denizens that in our mind conspire against our immediate survival.

The Hall of Human Origins visually underscores a suspicion that all the self-knowledge and organization of what we've discovered, all our speculations about "why" and "what," present no lasting proof of our inevitable triumph as a species. We've struggled to survive and have done so by ravaging our fellow travelers on this planet. We may have fought wars with each other, even tried to annihilate whole races, in our collective human story. But for all our divisions, we've united as the human family in our contempt for and fear of the animals who surround us and who've accompanied every loping step of our journey. Yes, we've also revered them and read their bodies to conjure up or determine the future. But we've also beaten them down, hunted them to extinction, or perpetuated their existence so we can end it when we wish. We've stuffed and mounted them, counted the bones and rearranged the fossils, and painted pictures behind them. We still have no idea who they are; and we still can't leave them alone.

Both the museum and the planetarium literally reflect on the past: looking into the strata of the earth and observing the orbits of the stars to show us what occurred many thousands, indeed millions, of years ago. We see the passing away as well as the continual cycling of life and death through the seasons. Although in some ways a whited sepulcher of Gilded Age expectations for the future of humanity, the museum doesn't shy away from the tooth and nail, bone and skin that are our only witnesses to the endless human desire to catalogue life and muse on its vanishing.

We cannot live in the past. Like animals, cultures come and go—overtaken by other species or brought down by climatic change and an exhausted resource base. Animals may die out for reasons independent of demonstrable human activity: disease and parasites invade them, predators consume them, floods and drought destroy their habitats. Conversely, progress *has* been made: to ignore the daily benefits that engineering, sanitation, medicine, agriculture, electricity, general literacy, and the internal combustion engine have brought to humanity would be perverse. We cannot turn back, no matter how attractive our imagined past may appear.

Even so, I'm not sure we've fully appreciated the self-organizing principles and cultural ecosystems of societies that didn't industrialize or organize themselves into larger entities. And those of us who stare out, like Gilgamesh, from the battlements at all we've wrought also cannot deny that our city walls have often been built at the expense of others' settlements and the destruction of nonhuman cultures and interfamilial organizations about which we still know virtually nothing.

So, having interred the past, those of us not yet buried by it look to the future and squint for signs of hope. Throughout the first eight months of 2012, the museum staged an exhibition entitled "Beyond Planet Earth." The show catalogued our ideas about the other planets in our solar system and displayed objects from half a century of space exploration. One of the final presentations consisted of a series of four panels that examined the viability of "terraforming" Mars. Given the prospect that the Red Planet contains water beneath the surface (an examination that the rover *Curiosity* was undertaking at the same time as the exhibition), it would be theoretically possible to release that water from the ground and over the course of centuries change the composition of the atmosphere. Within a thousand years, this chemical process would produce enough oxygen for plants to grow and humans to breathe without a constant artificial supply, and the planet could become our second home.

At each stage of the exhibit, the panels presented pointed questions, such as: What would happen if we introduced foreign bacteria into the ecosystems? Might we change the planet so much that we would lose the potential to unearth its history before we settled it and thus miss information vital to our survival? The final panel, which offered a diorama of forested hills, orderly fields of growing plants, and what looked like llamas grazing, asked us to consider whether this step would be the right thing to take: Would we destroy any local, bacterial life that may exist within the water beneath the surface? Should we not spend the trillions of dollars that terraforming Mars would require to preserve life and arrest climate change on Earth? How would it be possible to carry Earth's citizens to this new civilization? And who'd decide who would go and who would stay?

As I looked at the diorama I couldn't help being stirred at the prospects that the display laid out: that we might re-create life in the universe; that we might start again after so mightily screwing it up the first time; that after the final human beings are airlifted to Mars our polluted and wrecked Earth might be left for several hundred thousand years so its ecosystem could cleanse its rivers and soils, break down the toxins and plastics, crumble the steel and brick and nuclear waste of millennia of our ruination, and allow nonhuman life to thrive once more. I looked at the dioramas of Mars and, as much as I tried to resist the reflection, this nominal and *ersatz* son of Mars could see himself much as Marlow does in *Heart of Darkness*—staring at what he believes to be uncharted territory, allowing his boyish imagination to color in red what he takes to be blank space, and wanting to make his mark on and stake his claim to *terra incognita*.

For all its suggestive questions, however, the diorama didn't grapple with the toughest issues, which natural science couldn't answer. Once we'd mapped this new world, would we set up governments and establish borders, allocate mineral rights and patent laws? Would we carry on our exploitation of animal flesh and skin into another world? (The presence of llamas in the diorama suggested that we'd give it a go.) Would we fight over these resources as we'd done on the planet that twinkled several hundred thousand miles away? Would we create hierarchies and rebuild our civilizations on the backs of those brought to the planet to work rather than to think? How soon would we be held hostage to our very Earth-like, territorial-primate chest-thumping? Would the imagination and ingenuity that allowed us after hundreds of centuries of human development to conceive and carry out the creation of another world in space be negated by the same narrow-mindedness and appetitiveness that had accompanied us from the beginning and that led to the destruction of our first world? Would it be the tragedy of Gilgamesh all over again?

The elephants in the room on the fourth floor and throughout this book suggest that the odds are good that it would—not because we couldn't imagine a different way of relating to the planet and other species or collaborating with other members of our own, but that it was the *very nature* of our species to exceed its boundaries, divide itself and squabble, and exploit the weaker or more vulnerable. We'd done it before, tens of thousands of years ago at the end of the Ice Age, and we were doing it again. Why should the next time be any different? Our genius and failings existed in the same frail body and scheming mind. The same impulse to preserve and protect that had gathered and placed the bones in the case, had also placed them around the neck or within the sanctuary. It was a desire to make something memorable by destroying it and then lamenting its loss. It was our way of capturing a piece of time and space, harnessing a little bit of the magic of the nonhuman, and through killing it endowing our brief and unimportant existence with meaning.

＊   ＊   ＊

Shortly after Wangari Maathai left us in September 2011, it was learned that she wished to be cremated and not buried, and that she wanted to be placed in a coffin that wasn't made of wood. She'd argued in recent years that too many perfectly healthy bushes and trees were being killed when branches were severed so pilgrims could wave them about on Palm Sunday before discarding them. Better, she suggested, to celebrate Christ's emergence from the tomb not through honoring the dead wood of the cross but by planting a seedling to celebrate new life. She wasn't going to let another tree die for her, especially if she and it were to go up in smoke. With all the ambiguity such a phrase implies, Prof decided to teach her fellow Kenyans yet another lesson.

Using three different species of plant—bamboo, papyrus stems, and water hyacinth (the last being an invasive species in Lake Victoria)—a group of women wove a coffin, which was then taken to a Hindu crematorium in Nairobi and burned, a shocking decision for many conservative Christian Kenyans, who anticipate a bodily resurrection from the dead. It was typical of Prof that, even in death, she wanted to demonstrate to people that a different path was possible, one not hidebound by tradition, and to embody in her actions the argument that, in spite of her eminence, there was no reason why a tree, even if it wasn't a two-hundred-year-old sapele, should be cut on her behalf.

As befitting the many roles she played in her life, Prof was the recipient of a private Kikuyu memorial service in her hometown, a large Catholic mass in Nairobi, and a tree-planting ceremony at Freedom Corner in Uhuru Park (site of several of her battles to protect public space). At the public events, she was honored with lengthy speeches from Big Men—a few of whom had been, shall we say, wary of her when she was alive and were probably secretly glad that their Jeremiah was no longer around to tell them how they were harming their people and the country.

For me, Prof's gesture of conservation acted as one tiny corrective to the fearful visions of Gilgamesh and all that's followed. In her death, Prof caused one less log to be downed, and one more tree to offer its services to us, her fellow respirators. She allowed one uniquely shaped individual to be recognized among the mass of undifferentiated timber waiting to be felled. And she let one rooted, chlorophylled life continue to reach skywards—a cleanser of the ashes and green-tinted rebuke to the bone-house.

Discussion Questions

1. Do you come from a country that was colonized or one with a colonial history? How does your experience of that or your family match or differ from either Wangari Maathai's or Daphne Sheldrick's?

2. Did any of the information in the book make you reconsider any prior opinions you had about either woman—both during and after you finished the book? If so, how and why?

3. What does Africa conjure up for you in your imagination?

4. Can you think of an issue that, like the blind men in the room, you thought you grasped but in fact misunderstood? On reflection, how might you approach that issue now?

5. The author draws a connection between Western colonial activity in the early 1900s and the slaughter of animals today. Can you pinpoint any differences, either positive or negative, in your own society's

attitudes toward animals between a century ago and now?

6. When might it be appropriate to apologize for past political and racial transgressions in your own society? What might be appropriate reparation, if any?

7. Are there any books that you read as a young person or were taught at school that now seem outdated, but nonetheless made a great impression on you? How might one read such works with a critical consciousness today?

8. Do you agree with the man at the American Museum of Natural History that "magic is unlikely" as a way to describe animals' senses and consciousness? Discuss why or why not?

9. How might we stop the poaching of elephants and/ or the psychology of extraction that underlies the need to take animal's body parts?

10. Do you think we should colonize Mars? How might we go about ensuring that we don't make the same mistakes again?

Bibliography

Achebe, Chinua. *Anthills of the Savannah*. New York: Anchor, 1987.

———. "An Image of Africa: Racism in Conrad's 'Heart of Darkness'" *Massachusetts Review*. 18. 1977. Reprinted in *Heart of Darkness: An Authoritative Text: Background and Sources Criticism*. 1961, third edition, edited by Robert Kimbrough, London: W.W Norton, 1988, pp. 251–261.

———. *Things Fall Apart*. New York: Ballantine, 1959.

Adams, Carol J., ed. *Ecofeminism and the Sacred*. New York: Continuum, 1993.

Anderson, David. *Histories of the Hanged: The Dirty War in Kenya and the End of Empire*. New York: W.W. Norton, 2005.

Balcombe, Jonathan. *Second Nature: The Inner Lives of Animals*. New York: Palgrave Macmillan, 2010.

Bilger, Burkhard. "Beware of the Dogs." *The New Yorker*, February 27, 2012.

Christy, Brian. "Ivory Worship." *National Geographic*, October 2012.

Cobain, Ian, and Jessica Hatcher. "Kenyan Mau Mau Victims

in Talks with UK Government over Legal Settlement," *The Guardian*, May 5, 2013.

Cobain, Ian, Richard Norton-Taylor, and Clar Ni Chonghaile. "Mau Mau Veterans Win Right to Sue British Government," *The Guardian*, October 5, 2012.

Cobain, Ian, and Richard Norton-Taylor. "Sins of Colonialists Lay Concealed for Decades in Secret Archive," *The Guardian*, April 18, 2012.

Conrad, Joseph. *Heart of Darkness*. Harmondsworth, Middx.: Penguin Modern Classics, 1981. (This edition was used for the quotations.)

———. *Heart of Darkness* with *The Congo Diary*. With an introduction and notes by Robert Hampson. London: Penguin, 1995.

Dalrymple, William. *The Last Mughal: The Fall of a Dynasty, 1857*. New York: Vintage, 2006.

His Majesty's East African Trade and Information Office. *Kenya: Britain's Most Attractive Colony*. Nairobi, Kenya: His Majesty's East African Trade and Information Office, 1934.

Easterly, William. *The White Man's Burden: Why the West's Efforts to Aid the Rest Have Done So Much Ill and So Little Good*. New York: Penguin, 2007.

Elkins, Caroline. *Imperial Reckoning: The Untold Story of Britain's Gulag in Kenya*. New York: Henry Holt, 2005.

Florence, Namulandah. *Wangari Maathai: Visionary, Environmental Leader, Political Activist*. Unpublished manuscript, 2012.

Food and Agriculture Organization of the United Nations. *Livestock's Long Shadow: Environmental Issues and Options*. Rome: UNFAO, 2006, <ftp://ftp.fao.org/docrep/fao/010/a0701e/a0701e.pdf> (accessed December 4, 2012).

Freire, Paulo. *Pedagogy of the Oppressed*. New York: Continuum, 30th Anniversary Edition, 2000.

Gaard, Greta. *Ecofeminism: Women, Animals, Nature*. Philadelphia: Temple University Press, 1993.

Gettleman, Jeffrey. "Elephants Dying in Epic Frenzy as Ivory Fuels Wars and Profits," *New York Times*, September 3, 2012. Gettleman is quoted in "Slaughtering of Elephants Is Soaring Because of China's Demand for Ivory," by Mark Memmott, on The Two-Way: NPR's News Blog, September 5, 2012 <http://www.npr.org/blogs/thetwo-way/2012/09/05/160595798/slaughtering-of-elephants-is-soaring-because-of-chinas-demand-for-ivory> (accessed September 5, 2012).

Gowdy, Barbara. *The White Bone*. New York: Metropolitan, 1998.

Harrison, Robert Pogue. *Forests: The Shadow of Civilization*. Chicago: University of Chicago Press, 1992. The segment on Gilgamesh is also excerpted in *This Sacred Earth: Religion, Nature, Environment*, edited by Roger Gottlieb (New York: Routledge, 2004) pp. 69–72.

Hochschild, Adam. *Bury the Chains: Prophets and Rebels in the Fight to Free an Empire's Slaves*. New York: Houghton Mifflin, 2005.

——. *King Leopold's Ghost: A Story of Greed, Terror, and Heroism in Colonial Africa*. New York: Mariner Books, 1999.

Keller, Mitch. "The Scandal at the Zoo." *New York Times*, August 6, 2006. Keller cites the book *Ota Benga: The Pygmy in the Zoo* by Phillips Verner Bradford and Harvey Blume (New York: St. Martin's, 1992).

Kennedy, Kerry, and Eddie Adams. *Speak Truth to Power: Human Rights Defenders Who Are Changing the World*. New York: Umbrage Editions, 2000. The book (and accompanying website and film) is a project of the Robert F. Kennedy Center for Justice and Human Rights. The whole essay is available online at http://rfkcenter.org/wangari-maathai.

Kenyatta, Jomo. *Facing Mt. Kenya*. New York: Vintage Books, 1965.

Kheel, Marti. *Nature Ethics: An Ecofeminist Perspective*. Lanham, Md.: Rowman & Littlefield, 2007.

Leakey, Louis. *The Southern Kikuyu before 1903* (3 vols.). New York & London: Academic Press, 1977.

Maathai, Wangari. *The Challenge for Africa*. New York: Anchor Books, 2009.

———. *The Green Belt Movement: Sharing the Approach and the Experience* (New Revised Edition). New York: Lantern Books, 2006.

———. *Replenishing the Earth: Spiritual Values for Healing Ourselves and the World*. New York: Doubleday Image, 2010.

———. *Unbowed: A Memoir*. New York: Anchor Books, 2007.

MacDonald, Mia. "The Elephant Lady," *Satya* magazine, June/July 2006, <http://www.satyamag.com/jun06/sheldrick.html> (accessed June 18, 2013).

McGrath, Matt. "Fears of Forest Elephant Slaughter in Central Africa," BBC News, 9 May, 2013.

Merchant, Carolyn. *The Death of Nature: Women, Ecology, and the Scientific Revolution*. New York: Harper & Row, 1983.

Merton, Lisa, and Alan Dater. *Taking Root: The Vision of Wangari Maathai* (Marlboro Films, 2008).

Moyo, Dambisa. *Dead Aid: Why Aid Is Not Working and How There Is Another Way for Africa*. New York: Farrar, Straus and Giroux (2009).

Nagel, Thomas. "What Is It Like to Be a Bat?" *The Philosophical Review*, Vol. 83, No. 4 (October, 1974), pp. 435–450.

NBC News. "Report: Poachers Slaughter Half the Elephant Population in Cameroon Park," <http://worldnews.nbcnews.com/_news/2012/03/15/10707625-report-poachers-slaughter-half-the-elephant-population-in-cameroon-park?lite> (accessed August 8, 2012).

Noske, Barbara. *Beyond Boundaries: Humans and Animals*. Montreal: Black Rose Books, 1997.

Ochwada, Hannington. "Waiyaki wa Hinga." In *Holy People of the World: A Cross-Cultural Encyclopedia*, edited by Phyllis G. Jestice (Santa Barbara, Calif.: ABC-CLIO, 2004), pp. 905–6.

Orwell, George. *Burmese Days*. (New York: Harvest, 1962).

———. "Shooting an Elephant," in *The Orwell Reader: Fiction, Essays, and Reportage* with an introduction by Richard H. Rovere (New York: Harvest, 1984), pp. 3–9.

Pakenham, Thomas. *The Scramble for Africa, 1876–1912*. London: Abacus, 1991.

Price, Willard. *African Adventure* (1963). (The Adventure Series) (Kindle Locations 21-22). FourteenFiftyFour Ltd. Kindle Edition.

———. *Elephant Adventure*. (1964). (The Adventure Series) (Kindle Locations 2599-2600). FourteenFiftyFour Ltd. Kindle Edition.

———. *Safari Adventure* (1966). (The Adventure Series) (Kindle Location 3244). FourteenFiftyFour Ltd. Kindle Edition.

Riefenstahl, Leni. *Africa*. Berlin, New York, London: Taschen, 2010.

Roosevelt, Theodore. Quoted in "Teddy Roosevelt and the Indians," by Ojibwa, October 9, 2011 <http://www.nativeamericannetroots.net/diary/1093/teddy-roosevelt-and-the-indians> (accessed May 9, 2013).

———. TheodoreRoosevelt.com <http://www.theodore-roos-evelt.com/trafrica.html> (accessed May 25, 2013).

Rowe, Geoffrey. *Collected Letters*. Privately published, 2004.

———. *Soldiering On*. Privately published, 2004.

Rumi, Jalal al-Din. *Tales from the Masnavi*, translated by A. J. Arberry. Richmond, Surrey: Curzon Press, 1993.

Scully, Matthew. "Inside the Global Industry that's Slaughtering Africa's Elephants," *The Atlantic*, June 6, 2013.

Sheldrick, Dame Daphne. *Love, Life, and Elephants: An African Love Story*. New York: Farrar, Straus and Giroux, 2012.

Shepard, Paul. *The Others: How Animals Made Us Human*. Washington, D.C.: Island Press/Shearwater Books, 1996.

Siebert, Charles. "An Elephant Crackup?" *New York Times*. October 8, 2006.

Smith, Alexander McCall. *The No. Ladies' Detective Agency*. New York: Pantheon, 2005.

Smithsonian Institution Archives. "Roosevelt African Expedition Collects for SI" <http://siarchives.si.edu/collections/siris_sic_193> (accessed May 16, 2013).

Suroor, Hasan. "U.K. to Pay £20 million for Mau Mau Atrocity," *The Hindu*, June 7, 2013.

Swimme, Brian. *The Universe Story: From the Primordial Flaring Forth to the Ecozoic Era—A Celebration of the Unfolding of the Cosmos*. New York: Harper Collins, 1992.

Swimme, Brian, and Mary Evelyn Tucker (executive producers). *Journey of the Universe*, produced and directed by Patsy Northcutt and David Kennard, 2012.

Thiong'o, Ngugi wa. *Wizard of the Crow*. New York: Anchor, 2007.

Tingvold, Heidi, and Robert Fyumagwa, *et al.*, "Determining Adrenocortical Activity as a Measure of Stress in African

Elephants in Relation to Human Activities," Norwegian University of Science and Technology and Tanzania Wildlife Research Institute, February 12, 2013 <http://www.humanespot.org/content/determining-adrenocortical-activity-measure-stress-african-elephants-relation-human-activiti> (accessed April 11, 2013).

Wassener, Bettina. "As Affluence Spreads, So Does the Trade in Endangered Species," *New York Times*, January 1, 2012.

———. "Huge Seizure of Illegal Ivory in Hong Kong," *International Herald Tribune*, October 22, 2012.

Wikipedia. "The Uganda Railway" <http://en.wikipedia.org/wiki/Uganda_Railway> (Accessed July 12, 2012).

Wolfe, Cary, ed. *Philosophy & Animal Life* (Essays by Stanley Cavell, Cora Diamond, John McDowell, Ian Hacking, and Cary Wolfe). New York: Columbia University Press, 2008.

About the Author

 **MARTIN ROWE** is the author of *The Polar Bear in the Zoo*, *The Elephants in the Room*, and *The Bugs in the Compost* (all published by Lantern Books). He is the editor of *The Way of Compassion* (Stealth Technologies, 1999) and the founding editor of *Satya: A Magazine of Vegetarianism, Environmentalism, Animal Advocacy, and Social Justice*. He is also the author of *Nicaea: A Book of Correspondences* (Lindisfarne, 2003), co-author of *Right Off the Bat: Baseball, Cricket, Literature & Life* (Paul Dry Books, 2011), and the co-founder of Lantern Books. He lives in Brooklyn, New York.

About the Publisher

LANTERN BOOKS was founded in 1999 on the principle of living with a greater depth and commitment to the preservation of the natural world. In addition to publishing books on animal advocacy, vegetarianism, religion, and environmentalism, Lantern is dedicated to printing books in the U.S. on recycled paper and saving resources in day-to-day operations. Lantern is honored to be a recipient of the highest standard in environmentally responsible publishing from the Green Press Initiative.

www.lanternbooks.com